T0048999

THAT'S WEIRD!
BANANA PEELS WERE CONSIDERED SAFETY HAZARDS IN 19TH-CENTURY AMERICA.

NATIONAL
GEOGRAPHIC
KIDS
weird
but
true!
FOOD

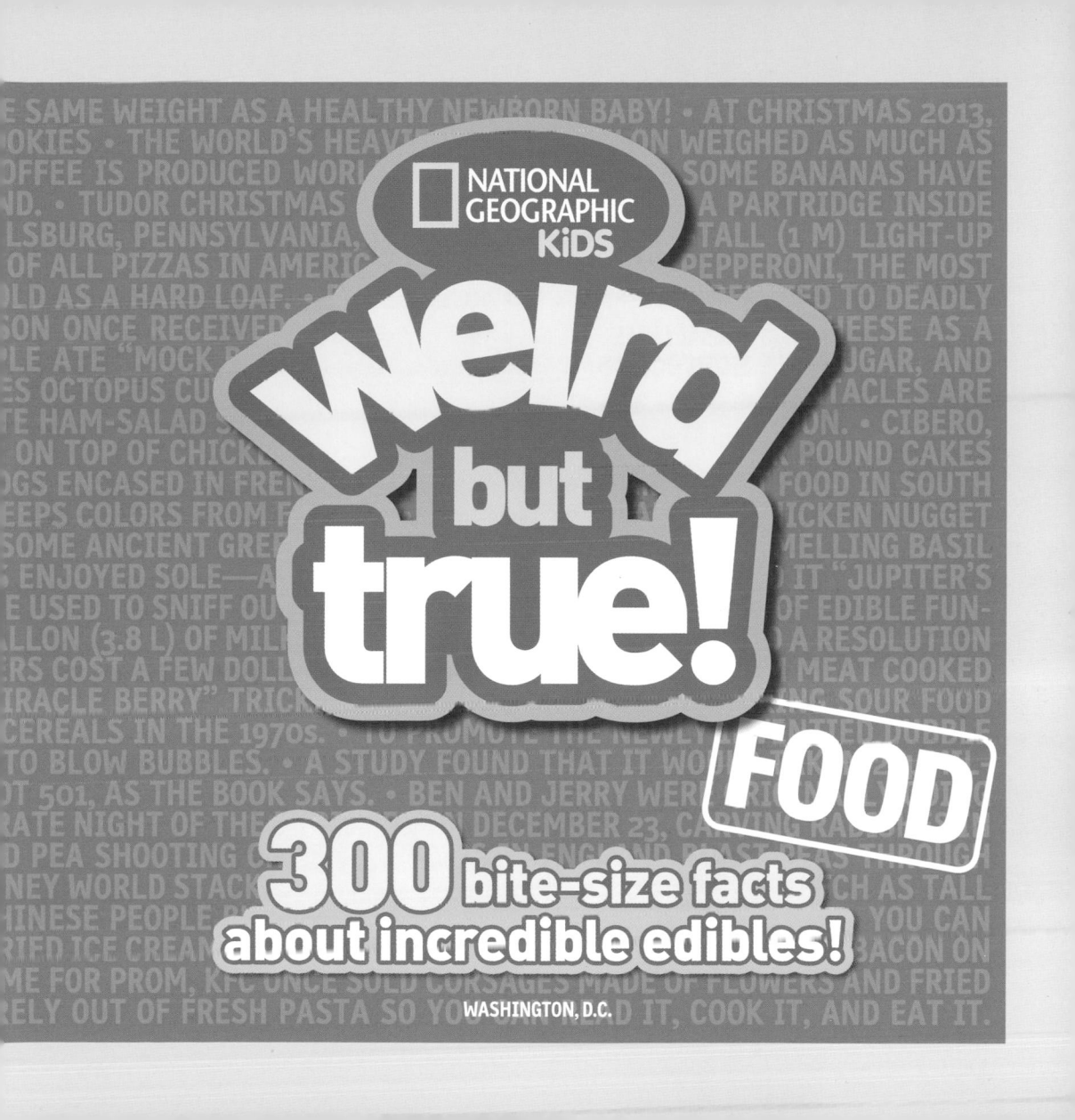
NATIONAL GEOGRAPHIC KIDS
weird but true!
FOOD
300 bite-size facts about incredible edibles!
WASHINGTON, D.C.

CALL ME SUPERCRAB!

A COCONUT CRAB'S PINCERS ARE STRONG ENOUGH TO CRACK OPEN COCONUT SHELLS.

EATING ICE CREAM MAKES YOUR BODY TEMPERATURE RISE.

WITH THE "TORTILLA BABY," YOU CAN DRESS AN INFANT UP TO LOOK LIKE A BURRITO!

LIME + KUMQUAT = LIMEQUAT

Cranberries get their name from their flowers, which resemble the head and neck of a crane.
EATING GARLIC CAN HELP FIGHT A COLD.
REFRIED BEANS ARE FRIED ONLY ONCE.

According to a recent study,
Americans
crave
cheese
more than
any other
food.

Sliced
grapes
catch
fire
when
cooked
in a
microwave.
DON'T TRY
THIS AT
HOME!

Sannakji, a traditional Korean dish, features **octopus** cut into pieces and served while the tentacles are still **squirming.**

Tomatoes are related to deadly nightshade, a very poisonous plant.
3-D PRINTERS may soon be used to make astronauts' meals in space.
Listening to high-pitched music notes makes food taste sweeter.

One year during prom season,
KFC sold
corsages
made of flowers
and fried chicken.

A BAND SENT A INTO SPACE AS PART OF A MUSIC VIDEO.

IN THE MIDDLE AGES, PEOPLE PUT
THYME SPRIGS
UNDER THEIR PILLOWS TO
STOP
NIGHTMARES.

Mayonnaise can be used to polish piano keys.

CHERPUMPLE=

a cherry, a pumpkin, and an apple pie stuffed inside a three-layer cake

CHERPUP

Rice
Krispies
ARE CALLED
Rice Bubbles
IN AUSTRALIA.

APRICOTS WERE ONCE KNOWN AS GOLDEN APPLES.

MYCOPHOBIA: FEAR OF MUSHROOMS

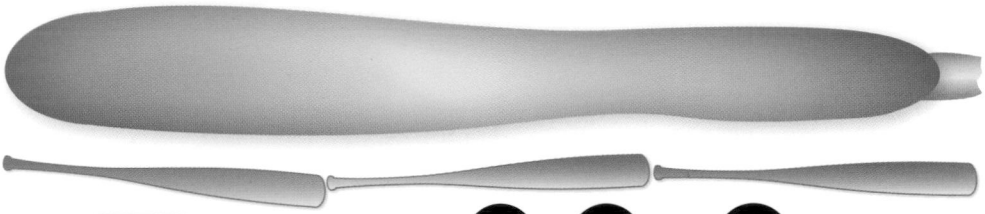

Zucchinis can grow as long as three baseball bats lined up end to end.

EVERY DAY,
MORE THAN
70 MILLION
CUSTOMERS
IN OVER 100
COUNTRIES
EAT AT A
McDONALD'S.

IT TAKES ABOUT
25
TOMATOES
TO MAKE ONE
14-OUNCE (.4 KG) BOTTLE
OF KETCHUP.

Black pudding
is a British
sausage — made of
oatmeal and
pig's blood.

COFFEE WAS THE FIRST FOOD TO BE FREEZE-DRIED.

"chyme" is the word for partially digested food in your stomach.

Ben and Jerry were originally going to make bagels, not ice cream.

THE WORLD'S LARGEST CABBAGE WEIGHED AS MUCH AS A ST. BERNARD.

LANGUE DE CHAT, THE NAME OF A LONG, THIN COOKIE, MEANS "CAT TONGUE" IN FRENCH.

WORCESTERSHIRE SAUCE IS MADE FROM VINEGAR-SOAKED ANCHOVIES.

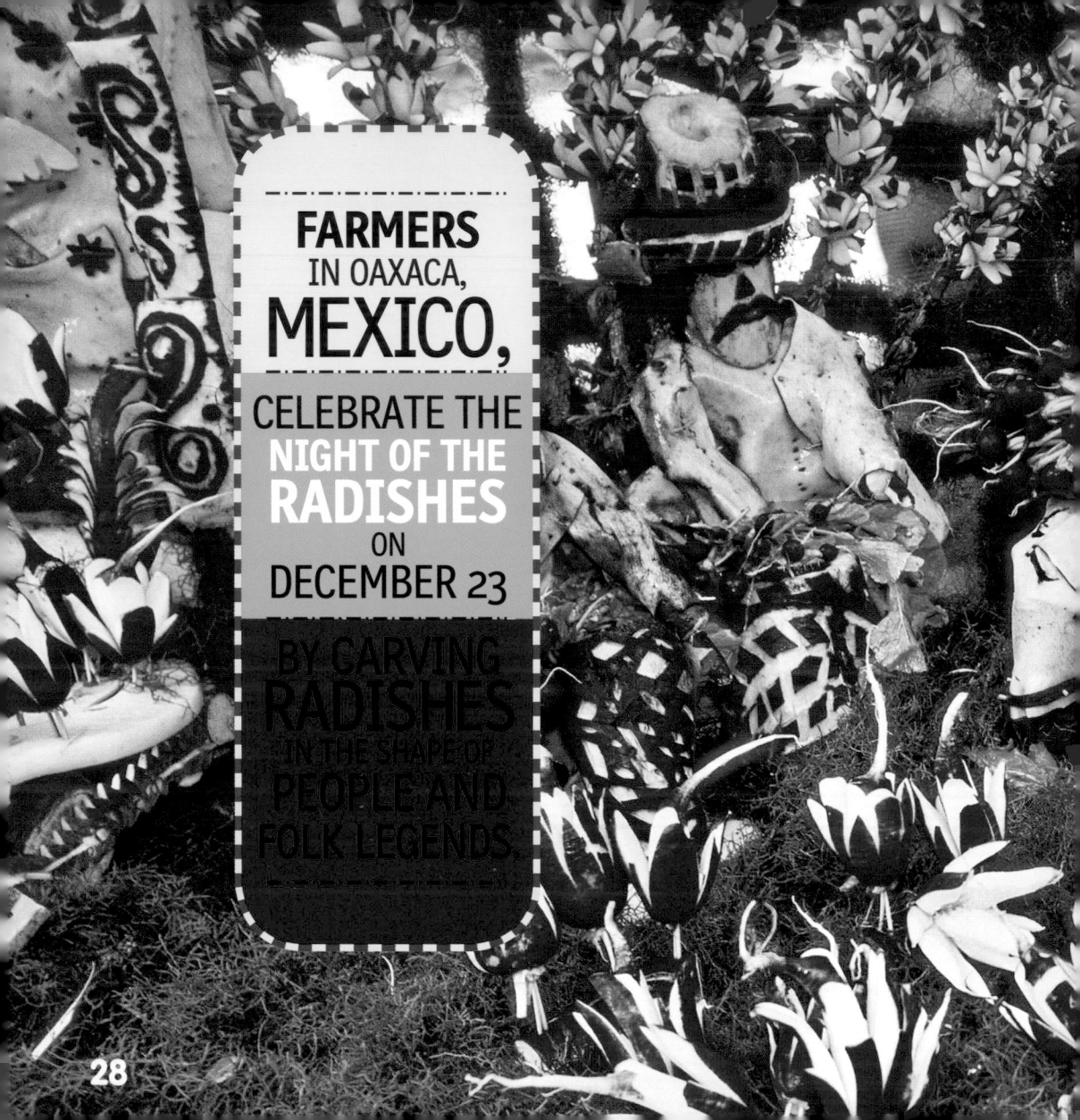

FARMERS IN OAXACA, **MEXICO,** CELEBRATE THE **NIGHT OF THE RADISHES** ON DECEMBER 23 BY CARVING **RADISHES** IN THE SHAPE OF **PEOPLE** AND **FOLK LEGENDS.**

With a price tag of $1,000, the world's most expensive cupcake contains 23 carats of edible gold.

CIBERO IS AN ITALIAN DISH MADE WITH COCKSCOMBS, THE FLESHY RED GROWTH ON TOP OF CHICKENS' HEADS.

TURNIPS CAN WEIGH NEARLY AS MUCH AS AN EIGHT-YEAR-OLD KID.

ORIGINAL
RECIPES
FOR

POUND
CAKES

CALLED FOR A
POUND
EACH OF (.45 kg)

BUTTER,
EGGS,
SUGAR, AND
FLOUR.

The human
stomach
can hold up
to half a
gallon
of food and (1.9 L)
water.

Classic scary movie star
Vincent Price
also wrote his own
cookbook.

Raw red **kidney beans** can be **poisonous** (but cooked ones are safe to eat)!

Scientists have created a **dairy-free,** plant-based **ice cream.**

USAIN BOLT, THE WORLD'S FASTEST MAN, RUNS THE 100-METER DASH AS FAST AS **KETCHUP SQUIRTS** OUT OF A **BOTTLE.**

YOUR TASTE BUDS LAST ABOUT 10 DAYS;

THEN YOU GROW
NEW ONES.

ICEBERG LETTUCE IS ALSO CALLED CRISPHEAD.

Ancient Romans ENJOYED sole, a flat fish, SO MUCH THAT THEY CALLED IT "Jupiter's Sandal," AFTER THE KING OF THEIR GODS.

ASTRONAUTS
NEIL ARMSTRONG AND
BUZZ ALDRIN ATE
HAM-SALAD
SANDWICHES
AFTER LANDING
ON THE MOON.

AN ARIZONA LAW BANS FERRETS FROM RESTAURANTS.

President Andrew Jackson kept a MILK COW on the White House lawn.

OLiVES ARE TECHNICALLY A FRUIT.

Smelling the herb **rosemary** can improve your memory.

The shells of **cashew nuts** can give people an itchy rash.

Edible tattoos may soon be used to mark fruit in grocery stores, instead of stickers.

SOME 70,000 GALLONS (264,979 L) OF BORSCHT—A COLD BEET SOUP—WAS SERVED AT THE 2014 OLYMPIC GAMES IN RUSSIA.

During World War II, when food was in short supply, people ate "mock bananas" made from boiled turnips, sugar, and banana flavoring.

AT A
RESTAURANT
IN TAIWAN,
THE TABLES, CHAIRS,
DISHES, AND DECORATIONS
ARE MADE OF CARDBOARD!

Ancient Romans ate **strawberries** to cure bad breath.

The **Carolina Reaper** is the world's **hottest** chili pepper.

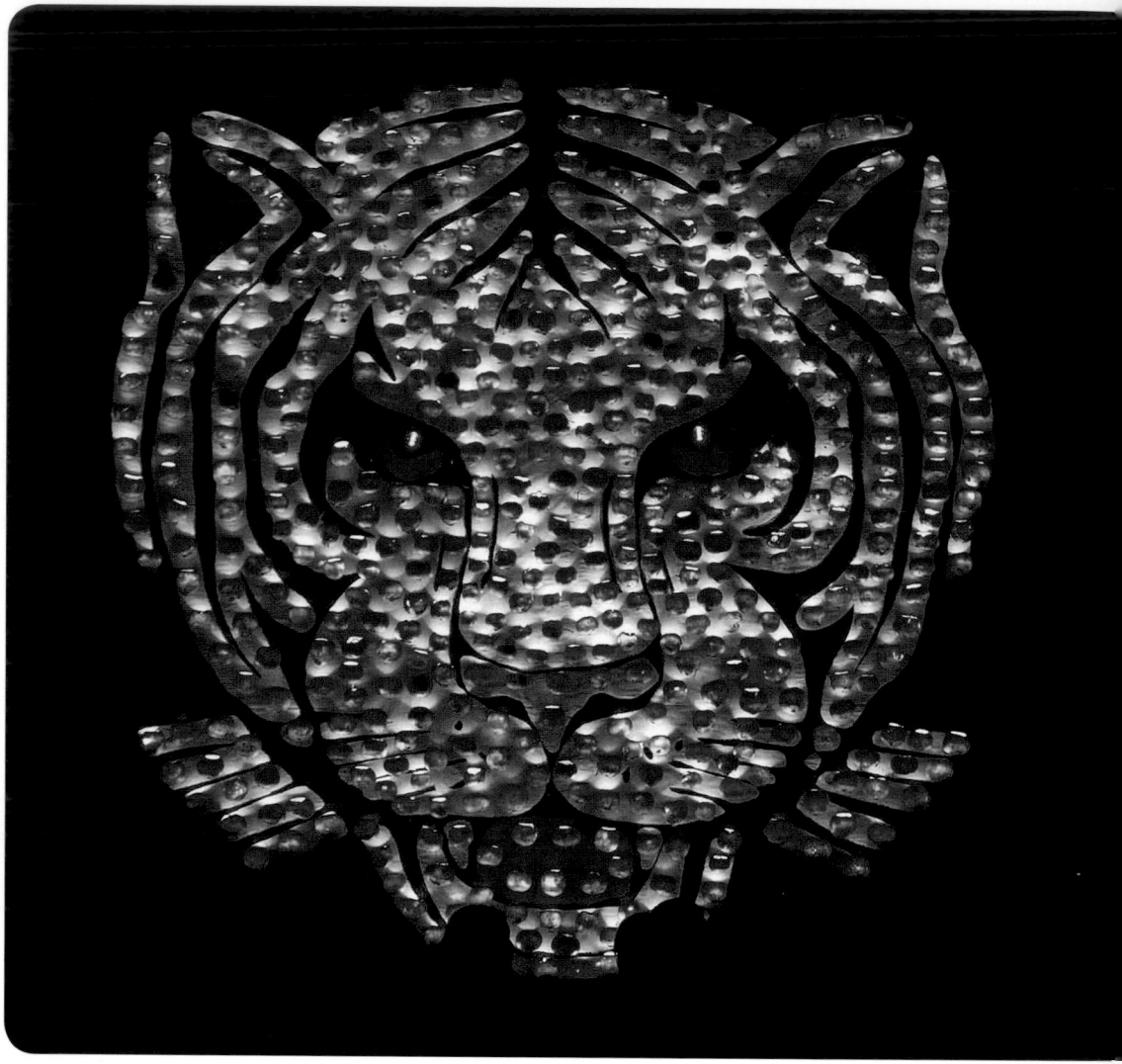

ABOUT
26 TONS (23.6 mT) OF
GLOWING HOLLOW TURNIPS
ILLUMINATE RICHTERSWIL, **SWITZERLAND'S**
ANNUAL **TURNIP FESTIVAL.**

Hot dogs
encased in
french fries
are a popular
street food
in
South Korea.

Washing
your clothes
with a teaspoon of
black pepper
keeps colors
from
fading.

THE 100 PLEATS ON A CHEF'S HAT ARE SAID TO REPRESENT ALL THE WAYS YOU CAN COOK AN EGG.

CASU MARZU, A TYPE OF CHEESE INFESTED WITH LIVE, WRIGGLING MAGGOTS, IS CONSIDERED A DELICACY IN ITALY.

An early version of Kool-Aid was called Fruit Smack.

AT A SUMMER FESTIVAL IN BARNESVILLE, MINNESOTA, U.S.A., WRESTLERS COMPETE IN A RING FILLED WITH MASHED POTATOES.

YOU CAN START A CAMPFIRE USING AN ORANGE.

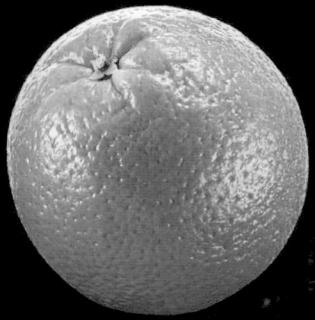

IN GREENLAND, A TRADITIONAL CHRISTMAS FOOD IS MUKTUK—RAW WHALE SKIN AND BLUBBER.

THE CHINESE WORD FOR CHOPSTICKS—KUAI-ZI—MEANS "QUICK LITTLE FELLOWS."

In Japan,
you can buy a
portable cooler
on wheels for a
watermelon.

The
cherimoya
fruit,
native to
South America,
tastes like
bubble gum.

CHILIES WERE USED TO CURE HEADACHES IN CHINA 2,000 YEARS AGO.

NORWAY FACED A NATIONWIDE **BUTTER** SHORTAGE IN 2011.

Happy New Year!

SPAIN: AT THE STROKE OF MIDNIGHT, EAT 12 GRAPES FOR GOOD LUCK.

MOBILE, ALABAMA, U.S.A.: SEE THE 12-FOOT (3.65 m) MECHANICAL MOON PIE DROP.

DILLSBURG, PENNSYLVANIA, U.S.A.: WATCH A 3-FOOT-TALL (1 m) LIGHT-UP PAPIER-MÂCHÉ PICKLE DROP FROM A FLAGPOLE.

LONDON, ENGLAND: ON NEW YEAR'S EVE 2013, BANANA-FLAVORED CONFETTI, PEACH-FLAVORED SNOWFLAKES, AND ORANGE-SCENTED BUBBLES FLOATED DOWN ON REVELERS.

GERMANY: EAT A GLÜCKSBRINGER, A MARZIPAN PIG, TO BRING GOOD LUCK!

AT BURGER KING IN JAPAN, YOU CAN BUY A "NINJA BURGER"
—A HAMBURGER WITH HASH BROWNS AND A SLICE OF HAM ON A BLACK BUN.

THE YARDLONG, AN ASIAN BEAN, GROWS TO BE NO MORE THAN HALF A YARD (.46 m) LONG.

AT A RESTAURANT IN NEW YORK,

WINNERS OF THE DAVEY JONES LOCKER CHALLENGE

EAT **2 POUNDS** (.9 kg) OF CRAB LEGS, **2 STUFFED** FISH FILLETS,

PLUS A **POUND** (.45 kg) **EACH** OF GRILLED JUMBO SHRIMP, STEAMED MUSSELS, AND FRIED CLAM STRIPS!

FANS OF THE
CHELSEA SOCCER CLUB
THROW CELERY
ON THE FIELD
TO TAUNT THE OPPOSING TEAM.

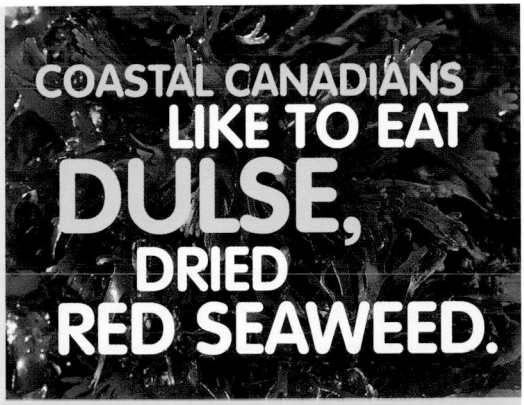

ENGASTRATION=

cooking one food

inside

another food

IN PARTS OF FRANCE, PIGS ARE USED TO SNIFF OUT UNDERGROUND TRUFFLES, A TYPE OF EDIBLE FUNGUS.

THE MOST EXPENSIVE TRUFFLES CAN FETCH OVER $6,000 PER POUND!

At the
Barbie Cafe
in Taipei, Taiwan,
meals are served by
waitstaff wearing
tiaras and
pink tutus.

A two-year-old slice of cake served at the wedding of Britain's Prince William was recently auctioned for $4,160.

DONUT + MUFFIN =
DUFFIN

A CANADIAN **DESIGNER** RECENTLY CREATED MINT-SCENTED **SCRATCH-AND-SNIFF** **JEANS.**

THE WORLD'S LARGEST PUMPKIN PIE MEASURED 20 FEET (6 m) ACROSS AND WEIGHED 3,699 (1,678 kg) POUNDS!

FOR $6,500, YOU CAN BUY A "CANDELIER,"
A LIGHT FIXTURE MADE OUT OF SOME
15,000 HAND-STRUNG ACRYLIC GUMMY BEARS.

Never cut
your noodles
in China:
A long noodle
represents
a long life.

IN A **SCOTTISH** HAGGIS-HURLING COMPETITION, PEOPLE STAND ON TOP OF BARRELS AND **THROW THE PUDDING** UP TO **217 FEET.** (66 m)

FREAKIES,
QUISP,
and KABOOM
were all breakfast
cereals in the 1970s.

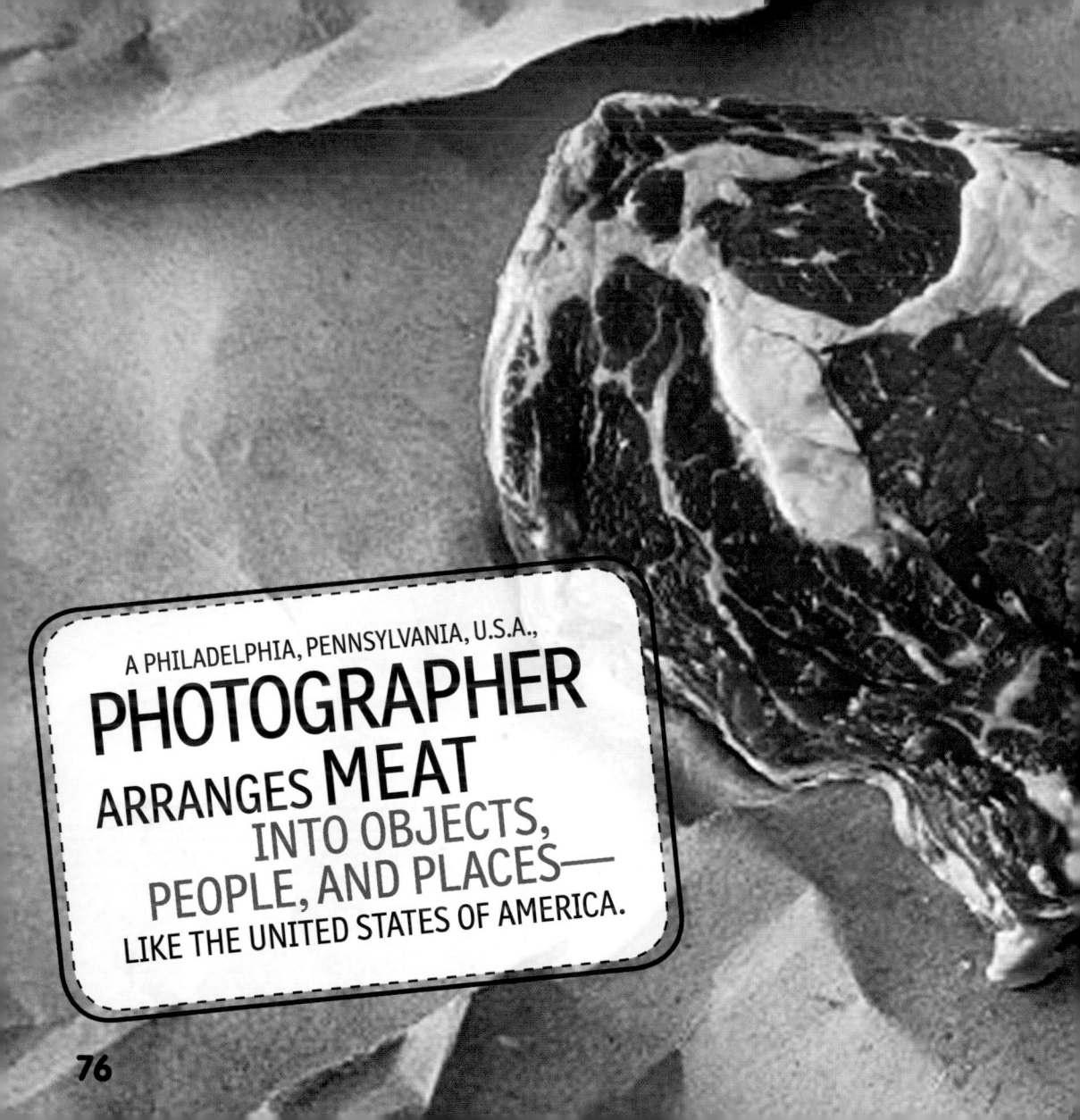

A PHILADELPHIA, PENNSYLVANIA, U.S.A.,

PHOTOGRAPHER ARRANGES MEAT INTO OBJECTS, PEOPLE, AND PLACES—

LIKE THE UNITED STATES OF AMERICA.

EVERY YEAR, MORE THAN
8 BILLION
SWEETHEARTS
CANDY CONVERSATION
HEARTS ARE MADE—
ENOUGH LOVE TO
GIVE ONE TO EVERY PERSON
IN THE WORLD!

MARCHERS IN THE ANNUAL **CHRISTMAS PARADE** IN BERRIEN SPRINGS, MICHIGAN, U.S.A., **THROW PICKLES TO SPECTATORS.**

Los Angeles recently passed a **resolution** encouraging people not to **eat meat** on Mondays.

RESEARCHERS FOUND PIECES OF **5,500-YEAR-OLD BREAD** IN A PIT IN OXFORDSHIRE, ENGLAND.

In the 1830s, ketchup was sold in pill form as a treatment for stomach ailments.

THE **WORD** USED TO DESCRIBE THE **COLOR ORANGE** CAME ALONG AFTER THE FRUIT WAS NAMED **"ORANGE."**

More than one-third of all **pizzas** in America are covered with **pepperoni,** the most popular topping in the country.

ALEKTOROPHOBIA: fear of chicken

Laetiporus mushrooms taste like chicken.

WARNING: WILD MUSHROOMS CAN BE POISONOUS. NEVER EAT MUSHROOMS YOU FIND WITHOUT HAVING THEM EXAMINED BY A FUNGI EXPERT!

In southern Africa, people catch, squish, dry, and eat giant caterpillars called mopane worms.

THERE ARE ABOUT **7,000 CHERRIES** ON THE AVERAGE **TART CHERRY TREE.**

In Australia,
"melon skiers"
put their feet in whole
watermelons and slide
down a tarp covered in
soap and squished
melons.

KENTUCKY
FRIED
CHICKEN
IS A POPULAR
CHRISTMAS EVE
DINNER IN JAPAN.

IT DOESN'T MATTER WHAT COLOR FROOT LOOPS YOU EAT; THEY ARE ALL THE SAME FLAVOR.

The world's largest chicken nugget weighed 52 pounds. (23.6 kg) That's 720 times the size of a normal nugget!

You can buy dill-pickle- or wasabi-flavored candy canes.

RADISHES WERE USED TO EMBALM THE DEAD IN ANCIENT EGYPT.

Scientists are working on inventing a plate that doesn't need to be washed.

THE COLOR OF THE TWIST TIES
ON BREAD LOAVES
IS CODE FOR THE DAY OF THE WEEK
THE BREAD
WAS BAKED.

BARBECUING IN THE STREET IS A FORM OF PROTEST IN BRAZIL.

A gadget that attaches to a smartphone can emit scents of different foods—like sizzling meat.

AT A RESTAURANT IN THE MALDIVE ISLANDS, THE DINING ROOM IS UNDERWATER, 16 FEET BELOW SEA LEVEL.
(5 m)

THE TOTAL SURFACE AREA OF YOUR **SMALL INTESTINE—AN ORGAN THAT HELPS DIGEST YOUR FOOD—** COULD COVER A **TENNIS COURT.**

It takes about **36 apples** to make a (3.79 L) gallon of **apple cider.**

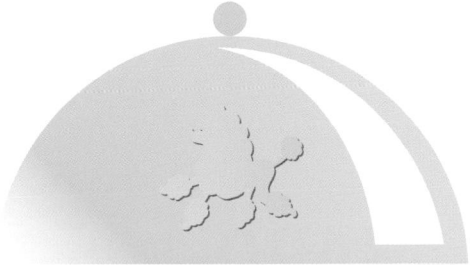

Pets Deli in Berlin, Germany, serves gourmet meals for dogs and cats.

The ice crystals in **Dippin' Dots** are 50 times smaller than the ones in regular ice cream.

HARD-BOILING A CHICKEN **EGG** TAKES ABOUT

12 MINUTES.

HARD-BOILING AN OSTRICH **EGG?** ABOUT

90 MINUTES.

ON THE INTERNATIONAL SPACE STATION, BOWLS AND DISHES ARE VELCROED TO THE TABLE TO KEEP THEM FROM FLOATING AWAY.

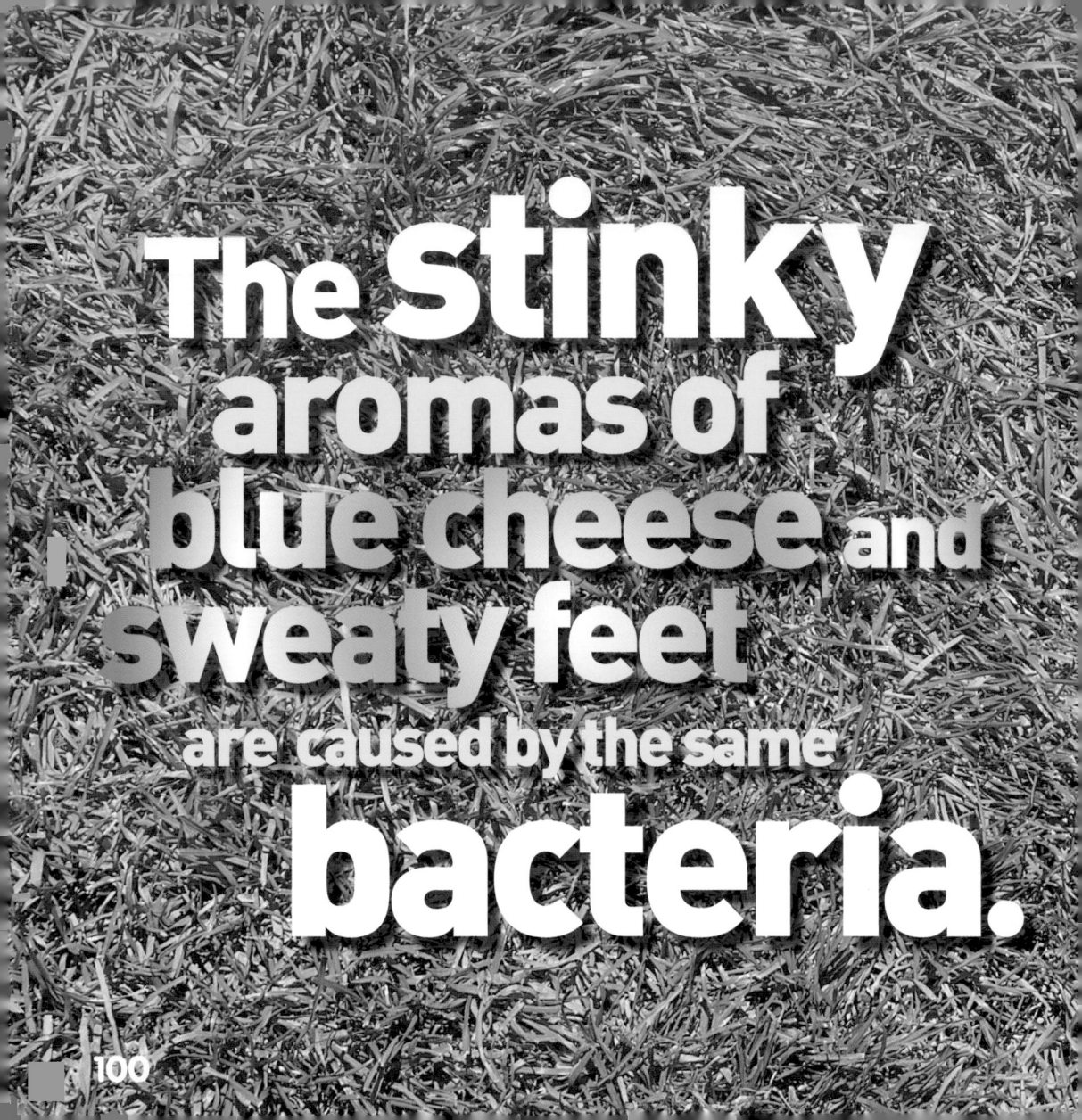
The stinky aromas of blue cheese and sweaty feet are caused by the same bacteria.

WHO YOU CALLING STINKY?!

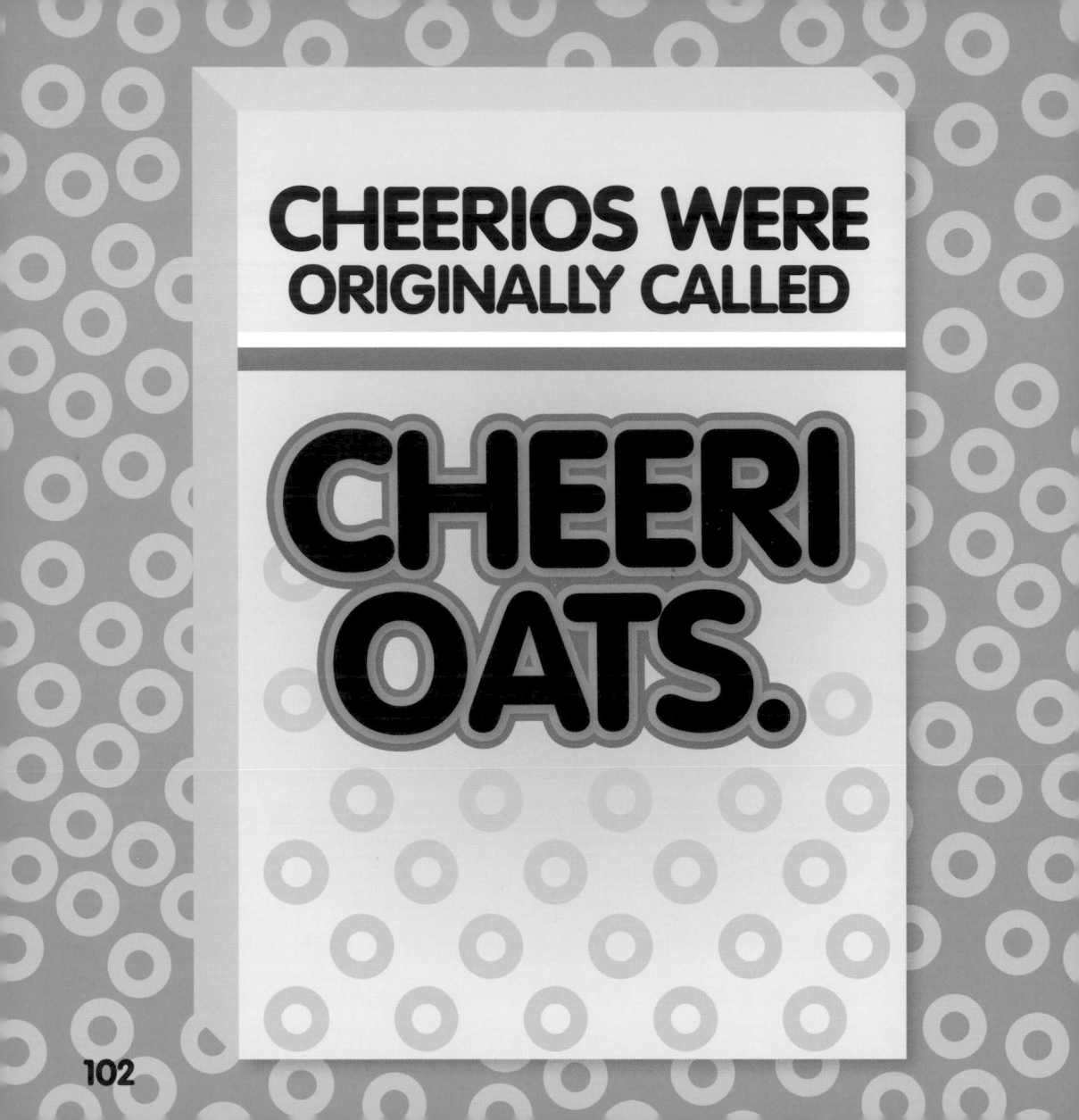
CHEERIOS WERE
ORIGINALLY CALLED
CHEERI
OATS.

A PHILADELPHIA, PENNSYLVANIA, U.S.A., RESTAURANT

MADE TACO SHELLS OUT OF BACON.

A survey of nearly 3,000 people in Britain revealed that the #1 breakfast annoyance is spreading butter that is too cold.

Using jellyfish proteins, a man invented a type of ice cream that glows after you lick it.

GOODUCKEN= A CHICKEN INSIDE A DUCK INSIDE A GOOSE

ADDING **BACTERIA TO CANDY** MAY ONE DAY HELP **PREVENT CAVITIES.**

YOU CAN MAKE JEWELRY FROM **DEHYDRATED POTATOES.**

400 years ago, English women decorated their hats and dresses with carrot leaves.

The West African **"miracle berry"** tricks your taste buds into thinking **sour** food is **sweet.**

A **YAM** IS MORE CLOSELY RELATED TO A **LILY** THAN TO A **SWEET POTATO.**

The peak time for **passing gas** is five hours after you've had lunch or dinner.

IN THE 19TH CENTURY, **WARRIORS** IN KIRIBATI, AN ISLAND NATION IN **THE PACIFIC**, **WORE ARMOR** MADE OF **COCONUTS** AND **FISH.**

A LEMON TREE CAN PRODUCE UP TO 600 POUNDS (272 kg) OF FRUIT A YEAR—THAT'S ENOUGH TO MAKE 100 PITCHERS OF LEMONADE!

The co-inventor of the cotton candy machine was a dentist.

A
HAMBURGER
MADE FROM MEAT GROWN
IN A SCIENCE LAB COST
$325,000—
ABOUT
100,000 TIMES
THE PRICE OF A REGULAR BURGER.

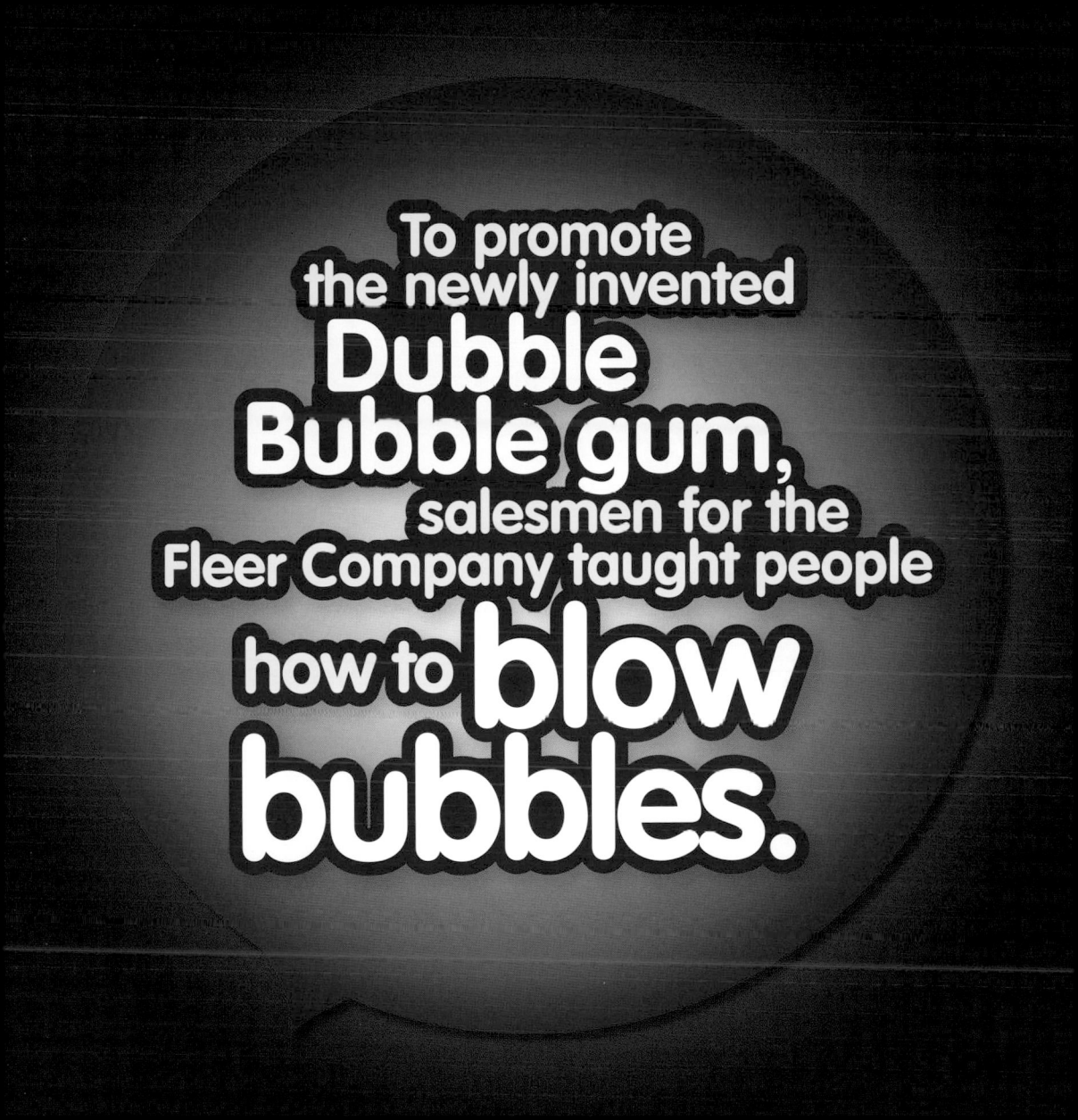
To promote
the newly invented
Dubble
Bubble gum,
salesmen for the
Fleer Company taught people
how to blow
bubbles.

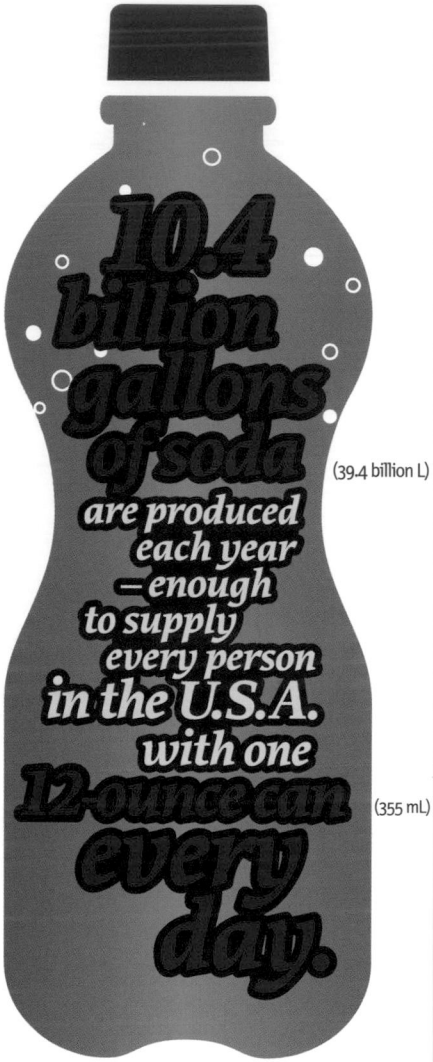
10.4 billion gallons of soda
(39.4 billion L)
are produced each year – enough to supply every person in the U.S.A. with one
12-ounce can
(355 mL)
every day.

The average Italian consumes half a pound of bread
(.23 kg)
a day.
1/2

THE LARGEST **HERSHEY'S KISS** EVER MADE **WEIGHED 30,540 POUNDS—** (13,853 kg) THAT'S AS MUCH AS ALMOST **3 MILLION** REGULAR KISSES!

A PASTRY CHEF ONCE MADE A 300-POUND (136 kg) REPLICA OF THE WHITE HOUSE OUT OF GINGERBREAD.

NEW ENGLANDERS EAT FIDDLEHEADS,
CURLED-UP FRONDS OF BABY FERNS.

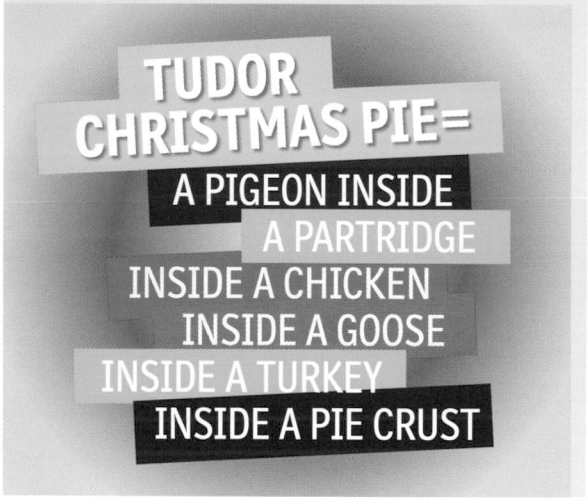
TUDOR
CHRISTMAS PIE=
A PIGEON INSIDE
A PARTRIDGE
INSIDE A CHICKEN
INSIDE A GOOSE
INSIDE A TURKEY
INSIDE A PIE CRUST

THE AVERAGE
AMERICAN KID
WILL EAT 1,500
PEANUT BUTTER
AND JELLY
SANDWICHES
BEFORE GRADUATING
FROM HIGH SCHOOL.

A BRITISH MAN SET A WORLD RECORD BY THROWING A **PEANUT** 124 FEET— (38 m) ABOUT THE LENGTH OF 3½ SCHOOL BUSES.

Baskin-Robbins once made ketchup-flavored ice cream.

TUROPHOBIA: FEAR OF CHEESE

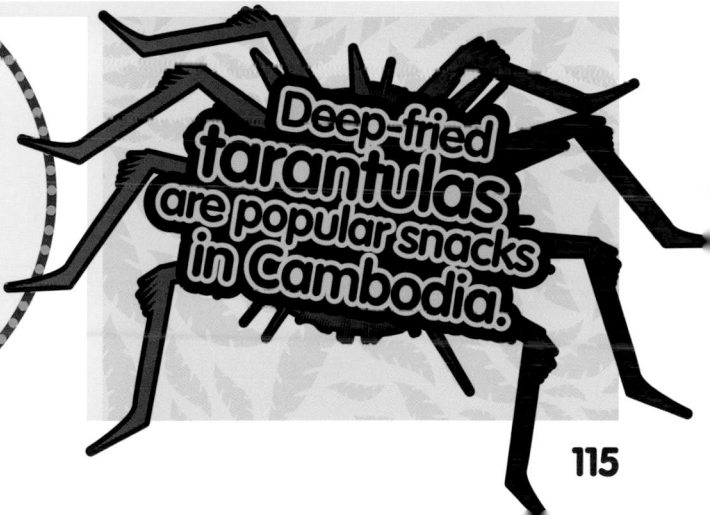

THE MARSHMALLOWS IN LUCKY CHARMS CEREAL ARE CALLED "MARBITS."

IT TAKES ABOUT

350 SQUIRTS

FROM A

COW'S UDDER

TO MAKE ONE GALLON OF MILK.

(3.8 L)

KNIFE + FORK = KNORK

SPOON + KNIFE = SPIFE

SPOON + FORK = SPORK

The world's biggest chocolate bar weighed 12,770 pounds— (5,792 kg) about the same as an African elephant.

THE AVERAGE AMERICAN EATS ABOUT 4,500 CALORIES ON THANKSGIVING—THAT'S THE SAME AS EATING 26 SLICES OF CHEESE PIZZA!

Food neophobia: fear of trying new foods

A CALIFORNIA MAN SET A WORLD RECORD BY EATING 69 HOT DOGS IN 10 MINUTES.

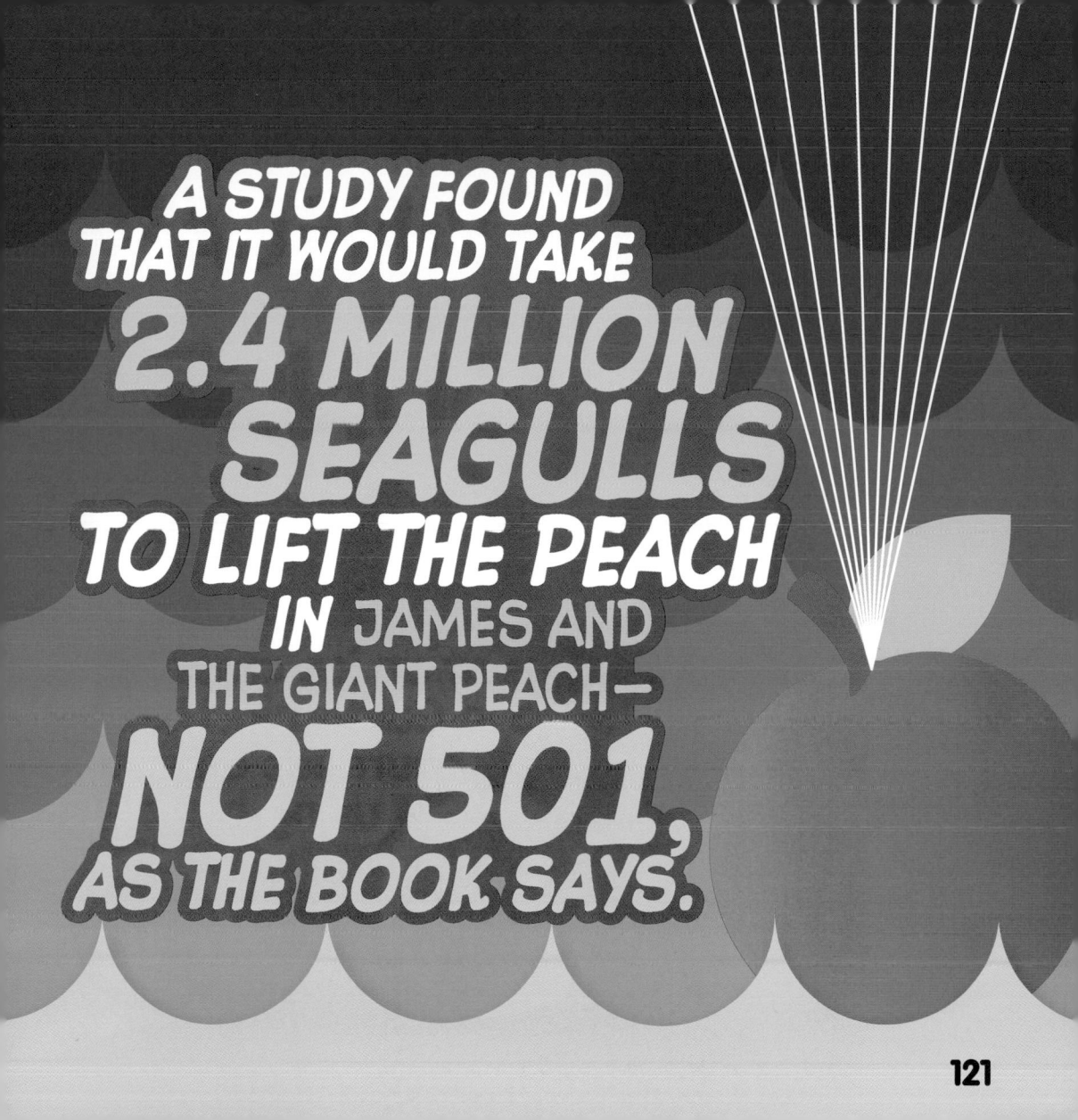
A STUDY FOUND THAT IT WOULD TAKE
2.4 MILLION SEAGULLS
TO LIFT THE PEACH
IN JAMES AND THE GIANT PEACH—
NOT 501,
AS THE BOOK SAYS.

CERTAIN KINDS OF
BALSAMIC VINEGAR
COST MORE THAN
$60 AN OUNCE. (29.6 mL)

Workers at an ice cream shop in California, U.S.A., churn ice cream using bicycles.

THE **CHANDELIER** IN THE **COCONUT PALACE** IN THE PHILIPPINES IS MADE OF **101 COCONUT SHELLS!**

A CAFE IN JAPAN OFFERS SOLO CUSTOMERS A GIANT STUFFED ANIMAL TO KEEP THEM COMPANY AS THEY EAT.

TO PROMOTE ITS PRODUCT, A BRITISH COOKIE COMPANY ONCE INSTALLED LICKABLE WALLPAPER IN AN ELEVATOR IN LONDON.

"COCA-COLA" IS THE SECOND MOST UNDERSTOOD WORD IN THE WORLD, AFTER "OK."

THE AVERAGE AMERICAN SPENDS 1.25 HOURS PER DAY EATING AND DRINKING.

IN JAPAN, THE McDONALD'S "CHERRY BLOSSOM BURGER" HAS A PINK BUN.

Cloud ears are a type of mushroom used in Chinese cooking.

A man in Israel grew a **lemon** the size of a **basketball!**

THE **MYSTERY FLAVORS** OF **DUM DUM LOLLIPOPS** ARE TWO REGULAR FLAVORS **MIXED TOGETHER.**

(THEY ARE CREATED WHEN ONE FLAVOR ENDS ON THE PRODUCTION LINE AND THE NEXT FLAVOR STARTS.)

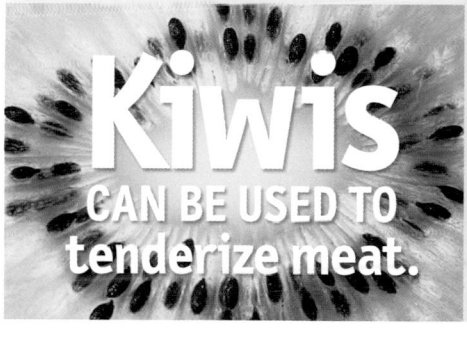

The Pillsbury Doughboy's name is Poppin' Fresh. He has a wife, Poppie, and two kids, Popper and Bun-Bun.

STARBUCKS COFFEE IS NAMED AFTER STARBUCK,

Some coffee shops pump artificial coffee scents into the air to entice customers.

A CHARACTER IN THE NOVEL *MOBY-DICK*.

Red is the most popular color of **gummy candy.**

UNTIL 500 YEARS AGO, NO ONE OUTSIDE NORTH AND SOUTH **AMERICA** HAD EVER TASTED CHILI PEPPERS, CHOCOLATE, OR **TOMATOES.**

IN A RECENT STUDY,

54%

OF THE PEOPLE POLLED ADMITTED TO

SERVING FOOD

AFTER IT FELL ON THE FLOOR.

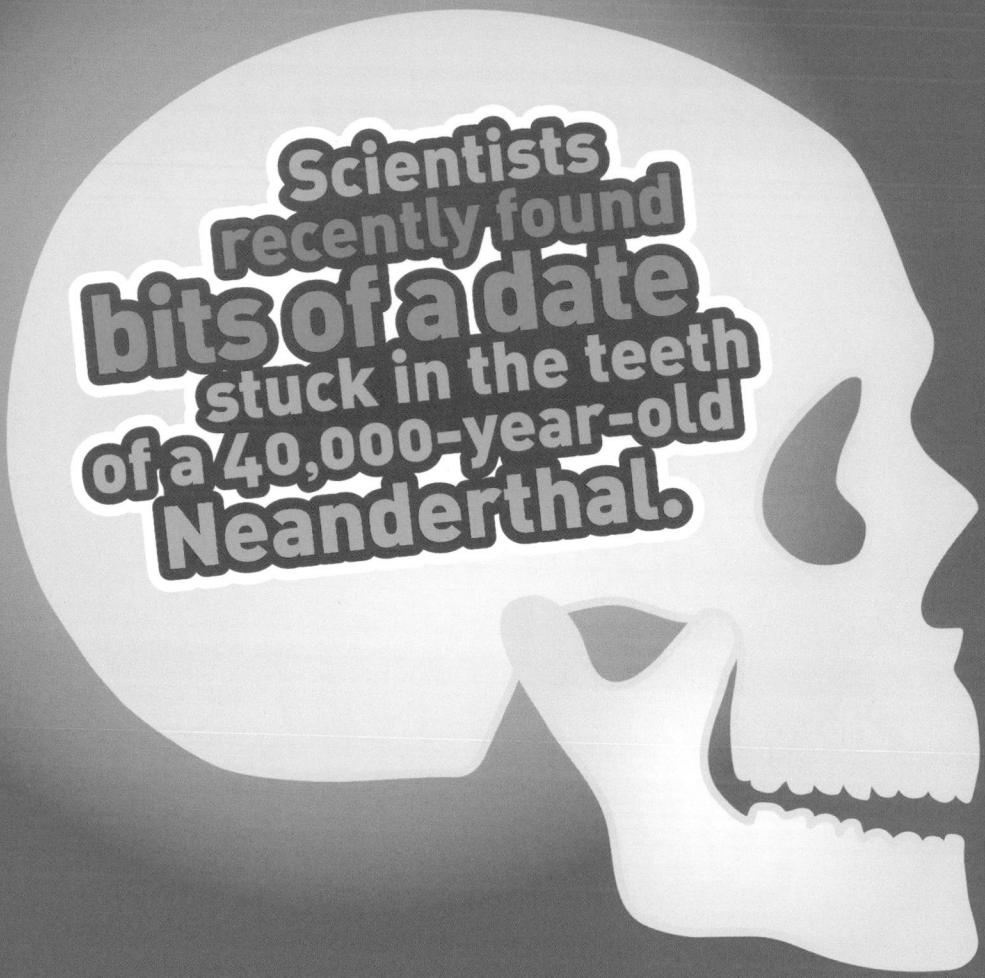

Scientists recently found **bits of a date** stuck in the teeth of a 40,000-year-old Neanderthal.

THE RESTAURANT CREDITED WITH INVENTING THE **HAMBURGER** HAS A STRICT "NO KETCHUP" RULE.

One copy of *Modernist Cuisine*, the world's most expensive cookbook, costs **$625.**

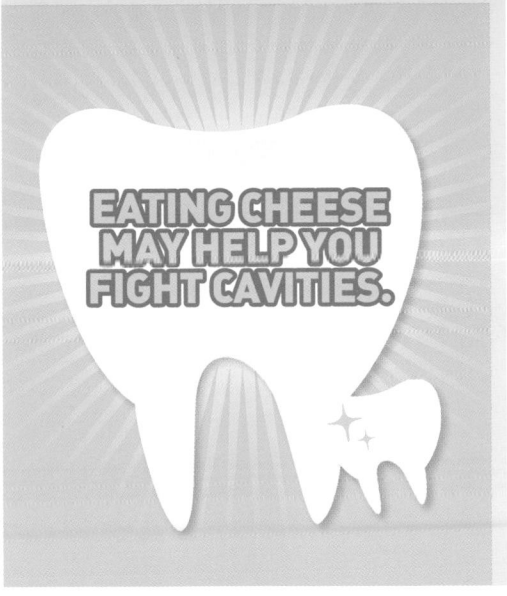

EACH BLUE STICKER ON A CHIQUITA BANANA IS PLACED THERE BY HAND.

AN AVOCADO HAS MORE

THAN TWICE AS MUCH POTASSIUM AS A BANANA.

AN 18-INCH-LONG (46 CM)

CORN DOG

SOLD AT AN ARIZONA BALLPARK HAS AS MANY CALORIES AS

9 PEANUT BUTTER SANDWICHES.

Coconut water has been used as a short-term substitute for human blood plasma.

You can buy smoked-salmon gelato in Rome, Italy.

Risktakers ARE MORE LIKELY TO **eat spicy foods** THAN THOSE WHO PLAY IT SAFE

Baconnaise, bacon-flavored mayonnaise, doesn't contain any bacon.

THE WORD *RAMBUTAN*—THE NAME OF A FRUIT NATIVE TO ASIA—MEANS "HAIRY" IN MALAYSIAN.

IN
WISCONSIN,
CHEESE BRINE
HAS BEEN USED
TO THAW
ICY ROADS.

IT WOULD TAKE RUNNING A MARATHON TO BURN OFF ALL THE CALORIES IN TWO FAST-FOOD MEALS.

ON THE INTERNATIONAL SPACE STATION, 93 PERCENT OF THE ASTRONAUTS' SWEAT AND URINE IS RECYCLED INTO DRINKING WATER.

THAT'S WEIRD!
K. NYBERG
K. HARBERT
esa

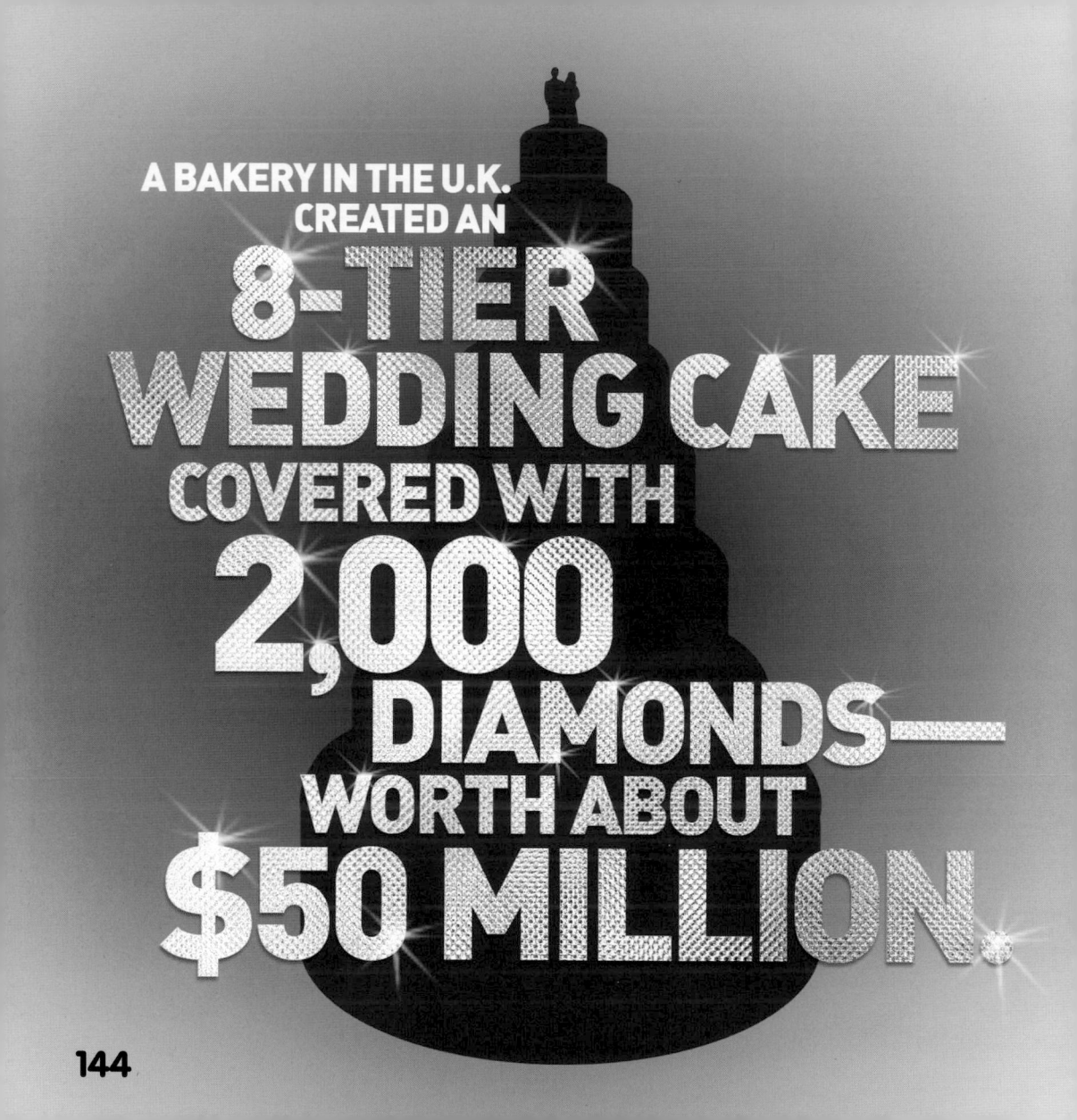
A BAKERY IN THE U.K. CREATED AN
8-TIER WEDDING CAKE
COVERED WITH
2,000 DIAMONDS—
WORTH ABOUT
$50 MILLION.

IN SINGAPORE, YOU CAN BUY HOT MASHED POTATOES OUT OF A VENDING MACHINE.

VISITORS CAN MAKE THEIR OWN

"FRESH" NOODLE SOUP

AT THE MOMOFUKU ANDO INSTANT RAMEN MUSEUM

IN OSAKA, JAPAN.

There are enough marshmallow Peeps made every year to circle the globe twice.

THE WORLD'S **LOUDEST RECORDED BURP** WAS LOUDER THAN A HAND DRILL.

Almost 4,000 years ago, ancient Chinese people buried hunks of cheese with the dead.

RHUBARB
IS ONE OF THE MOST
POISONOUS
PLANTS
TO DOGS.

ONIONS ARE POISONOUS TO CATS!

A New Jersey, U.S.A.,
museum is home
to a collection of over
5,400
spoons!

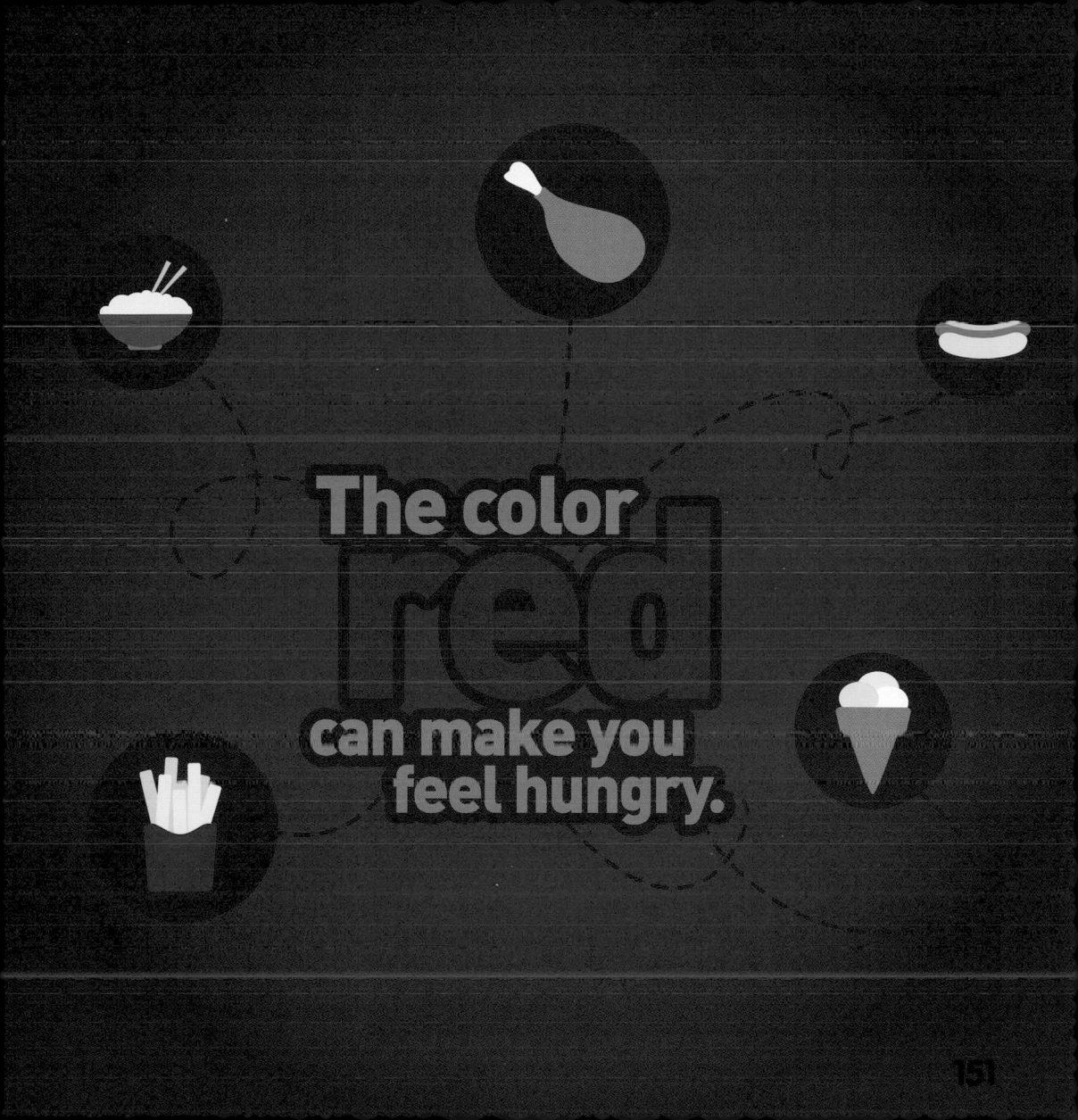
The color
red
can make you
feel hungry.

Miners traded gold for potatoes during the California gold rush.

THE WAIT LIST TO EAT AT A RESTAURANT IN EARLTON, NEW YORK, U.S.A., IS 10 YEARS LONG.

ON AVERAGE, AMERICANS EAT ABOUT 15 POUNDS (6.8 kg) OF CEREAL A YEAR.

A MAN ONCE ATE 233 RAW OYSTERS IN THREE MINUTES.

Ancient Greeks believed mint could cure hiccups.

An Oreo vending machine once dispensed 3-D printed cookies to customers.

BRUSSELS SPROUTS

KALE

BRUSSELS
KALE

AN **ISRAELI ARTIST** CREATES MINIATURE

REPLICAS OF FOOD

THAT ARE **12 TIMES** SMALLER THAN THE REAL THING.

In the U.K., **waffle fries** can be made in **social media shapes,** like **hashtags, emoticons,** and **@ signs.**

KIDS WHO LIKE SWEET FOODS BETTER THAN SALTY ONES TEND TO BE TALLER FOR THEIR AGE.

U.S. ARMY **SCIENTISTS** INVENTED A **PIZZA** THAT CAN BE STORED AT ROOM TEMPERATURE **FOR THREE YEARS** WITHOUT GOING BAD.

Mangoes are related to pistachios—and **poison ivy.**

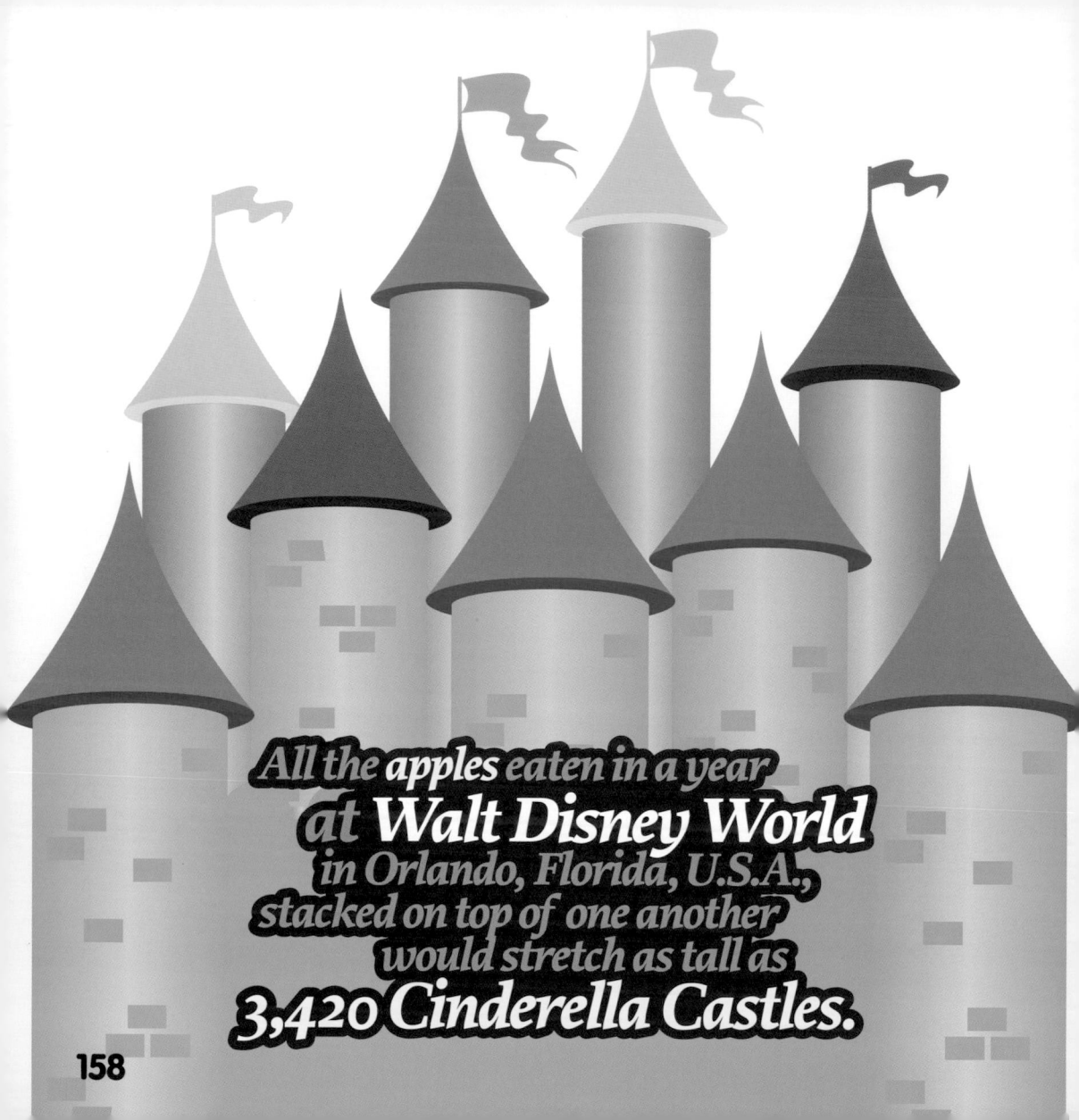
All the apples eaten in a year
at Walt Disney World
in Orlando, Florida, U.S.A.,
stacked on top of one another
would stretch as tall as
3,420 Cinderella Castles.

A JAPANESE DESIGNER CREATES EDIBLE PLATES, BOWLS, AND CHOPSTICKS USING A SPECIAL KIND OF BISCUIT DOUGH.

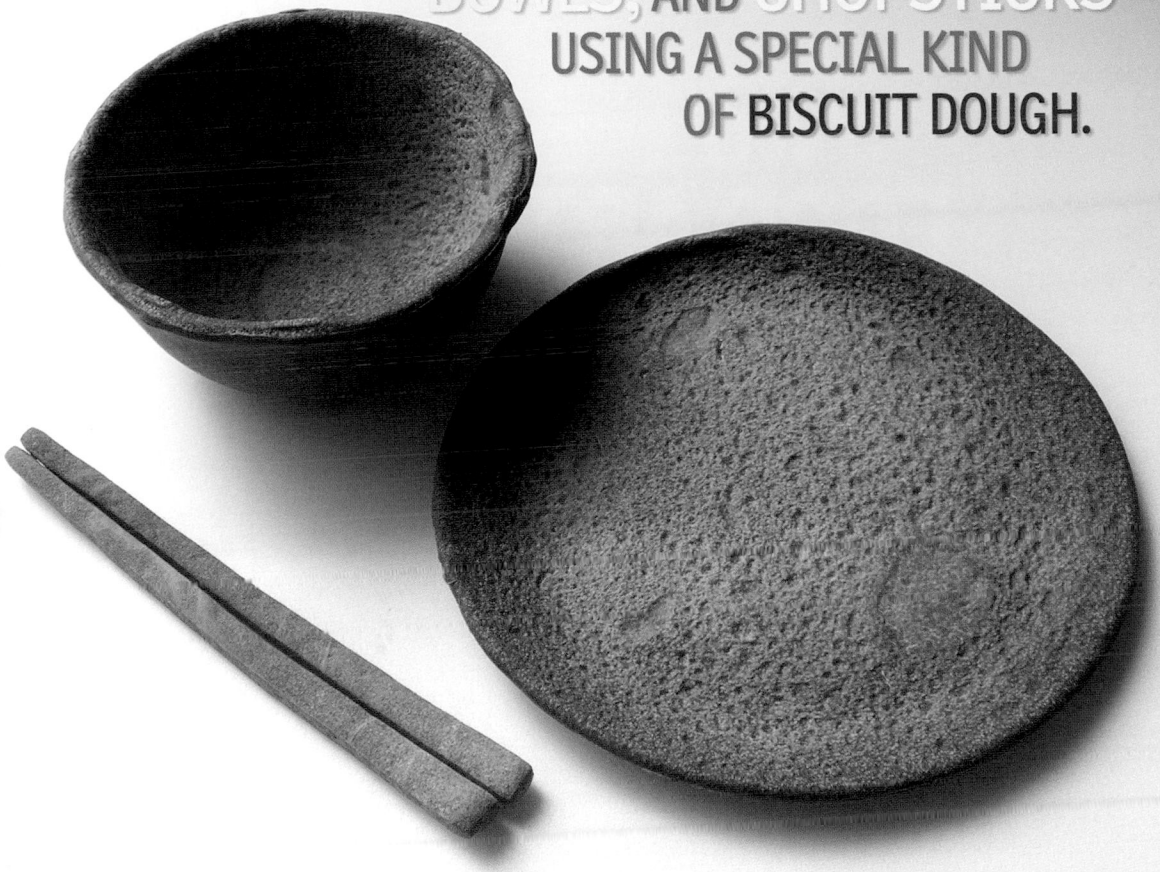

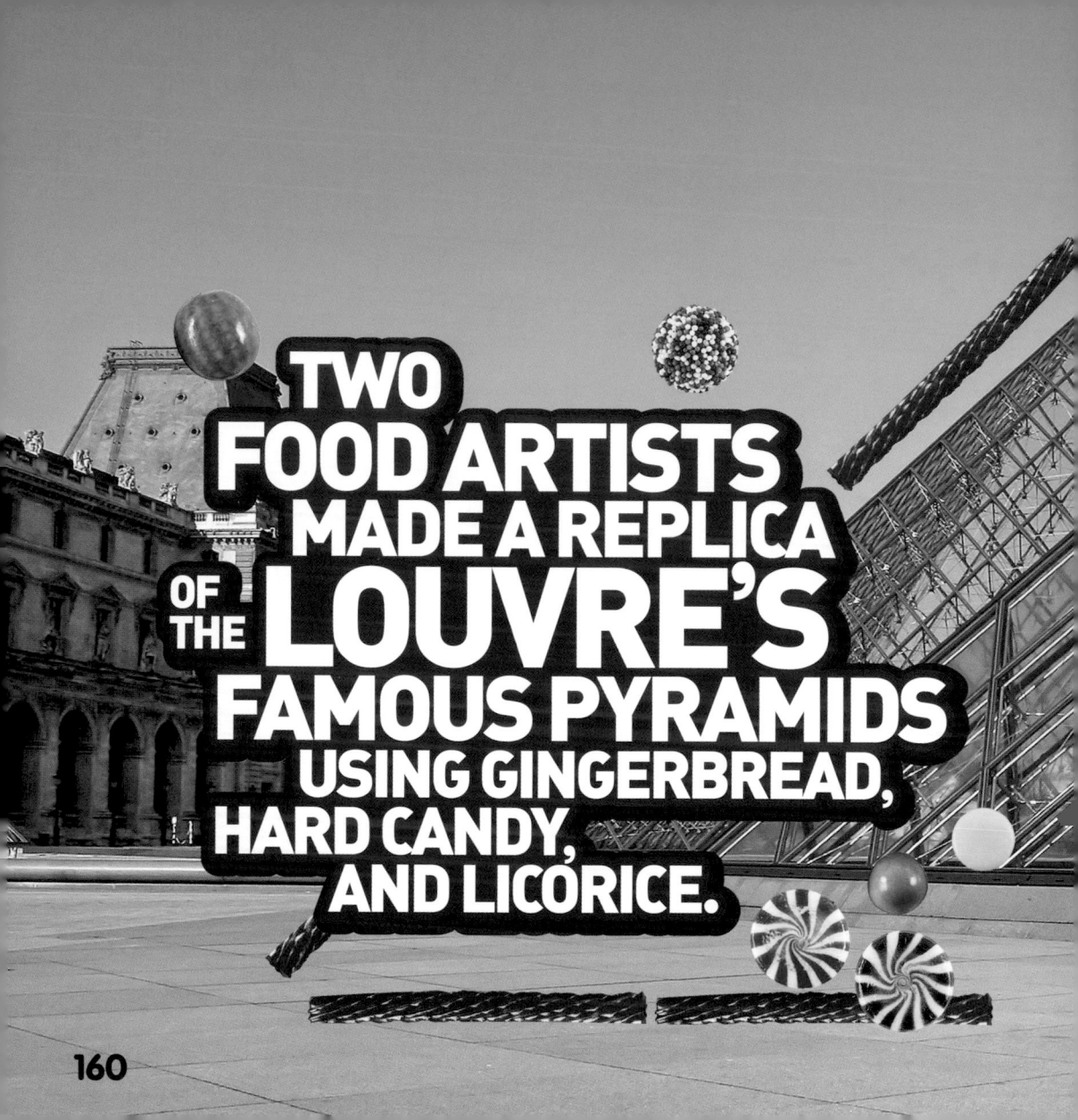
TWO FOOD ARTISTS MADE A REPLICA OF THE LOUVRE'S FAMOUS PYRAMIDS USING GINGERBREAD, HARD CANDY, AND LICORICE.

TO GET PERFECTLY EVEN SLICES OF PIZZA, YOU CAN BUY A LASER-GUIDED CUTTER.

A restaurant in New Zealand shoots burgers to customers' tables through clear tubes at 87 (140 km/h) miles an hour.

The potato chip was invented in 1853 by George Crum.

25 PERCENT OF ALL GIRL SCOUT COOKIES SALES ARE THIN MINTS.

ASPARAGUS STALKS CAN GROW 10 INCHES IN ONE DAY.
(25.4 cm)

16TH-CENTURY ITALIAN PAINTER GIUSEPPE ARCIMBOLDO PAINTED FRUITS AND VEGETABLES TO LOOK LIKE HUMAN FACES.

IN COLONIAL AMERICA, FRUIT SELLERS RENTED PINEAPPLES TO USE AS CENTERPIECES.

You can buy a candle that smells like a hamburger.

In ancient Egypt, baskets of onions were given as funeral offerings.

MOST AMERICANS REGULARLY EAT FEWER THAN 30 DIFFERENT FOODS.

SWEET POTATOES COME NOT ONLY IN ORANGE, BUT ALSO IN WHITE, YELLOW, RED, AND PURPLE.

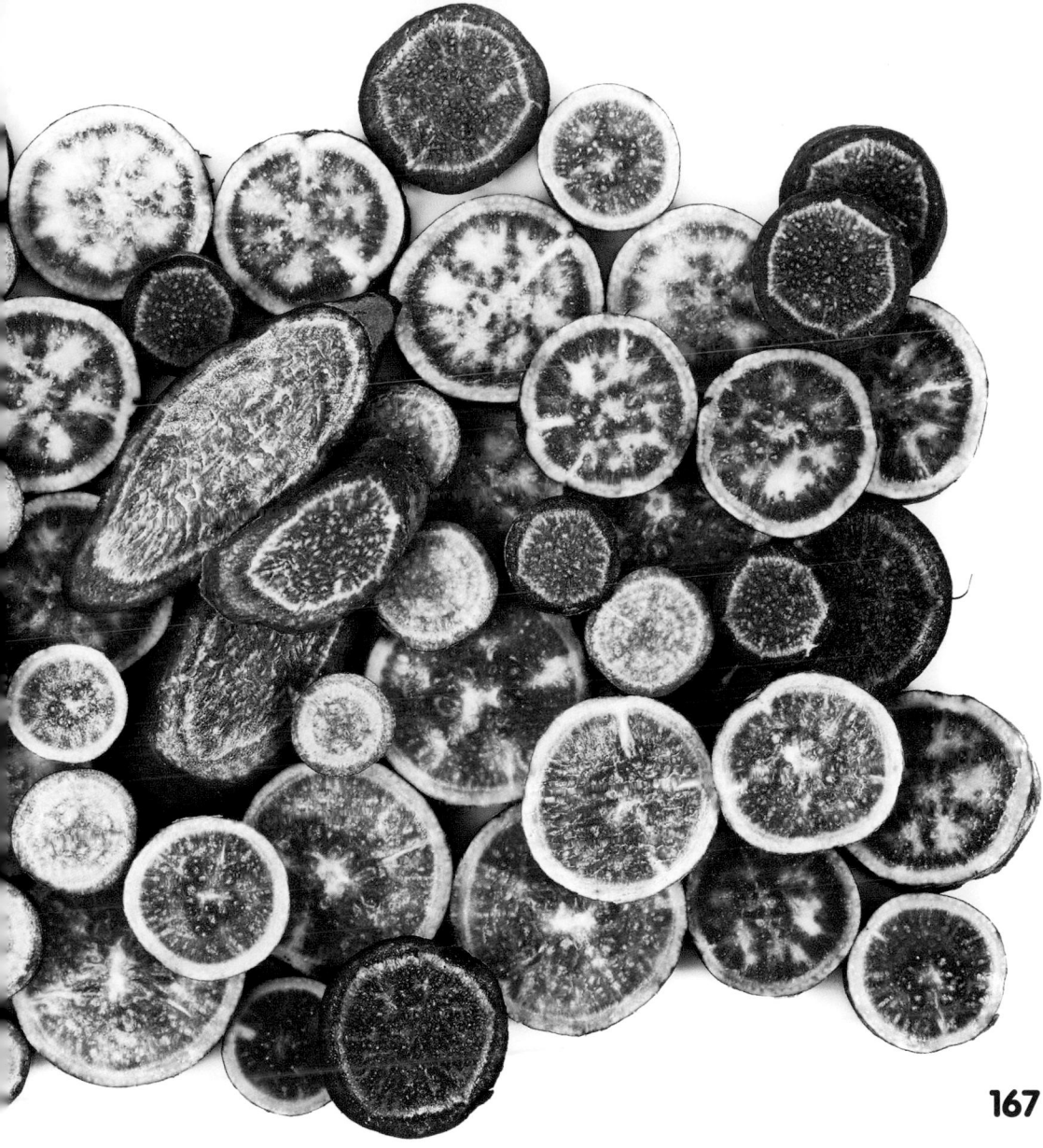

YOU MIGHT NEED A **TOOTHPICK** TO GET RID OF A **TOOTHPACK,** THE FOOD THAT GETS **STUCK** IN YOUR MOLARS.

CHERRY BLOSSOM, SWEET POTATO, AND BLACK SESAME SEED ARE ALL POPULAR ICE CREAM FLAVORS IN JAPAN.

The world's heaviest tomato (3.51 kg) weighed 7 pounds, 12 ounces—the same weight as a healthy newborn baby!

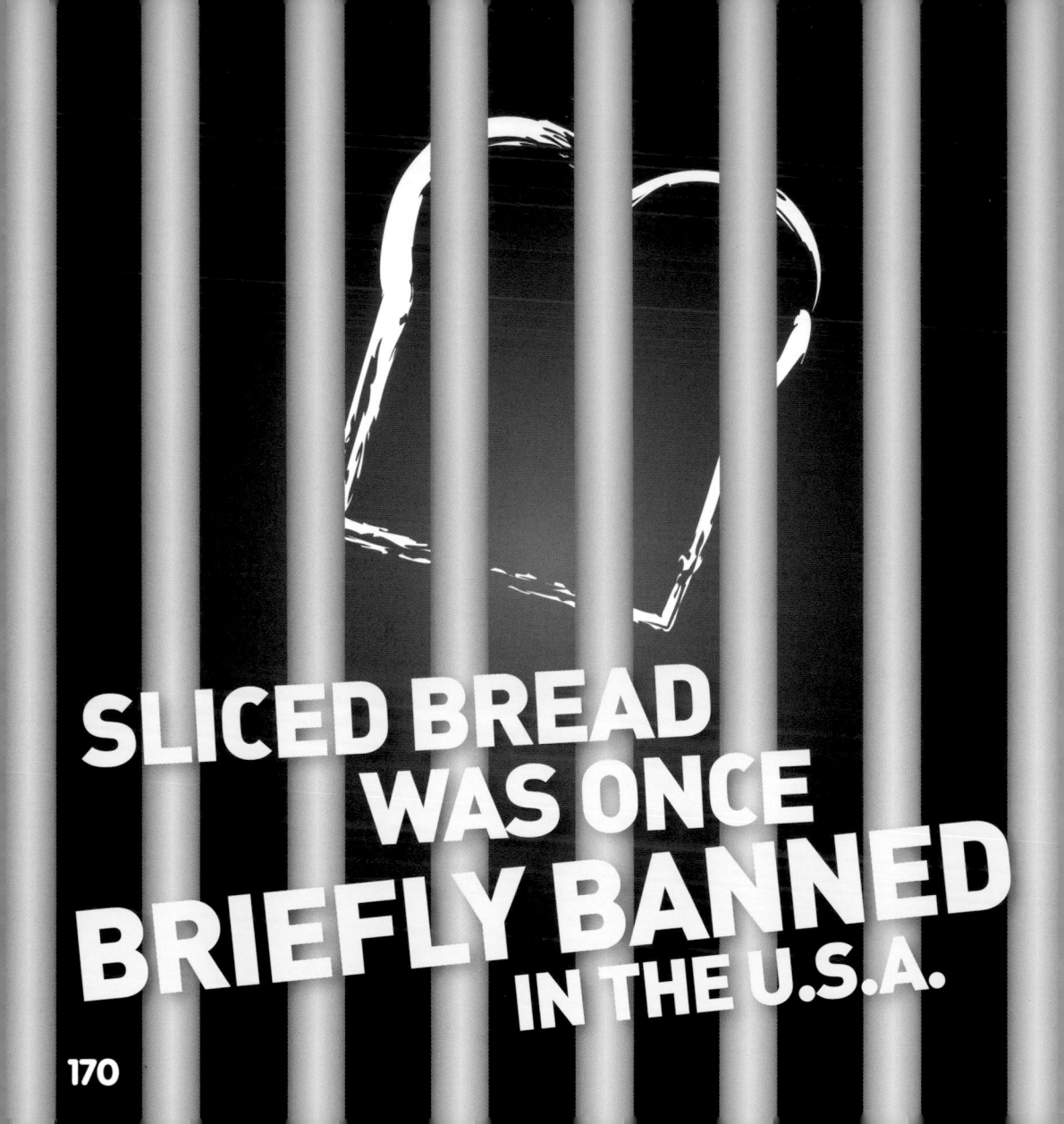

SLICED BREAD WAS ONCE BRIEFLY BANNED IN THE U.S.A.

A BAKERY IN

NEW YORK CITY

SOLD PUMPKIN DONUTS WITH TURKEY AND GRAVY FILLING

DURING THANKSGIVING SEASON.

75,000 crocus flowers are needed to harvest just **one pound** (.45 kg) of **saffron,** the world's most expensive **spice.**

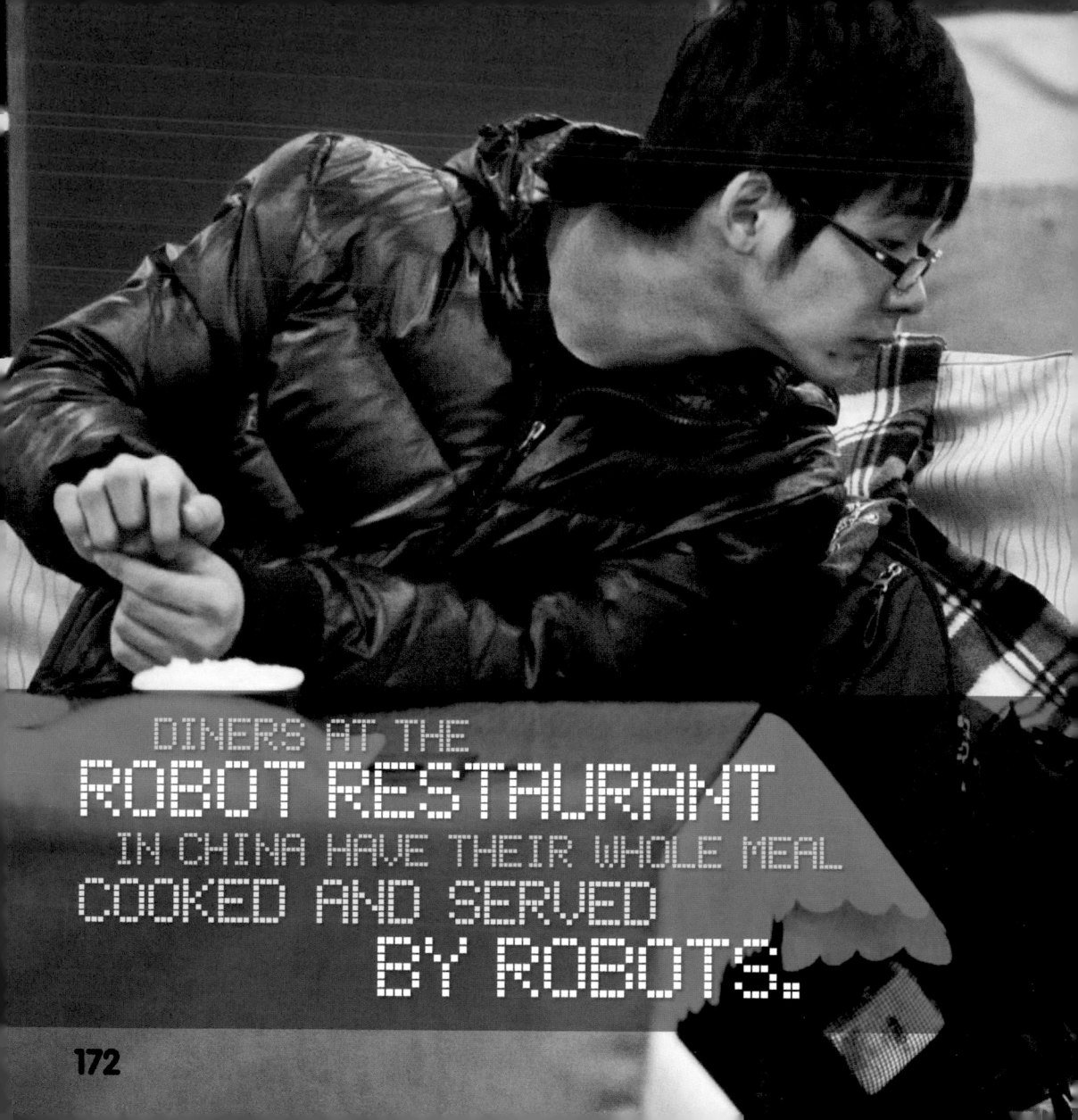

DINERS AT THE
ROBOT RESTAURANT
IN CHINA HAVE THEIR WHOLE MEAL
COOKED AND SERVED
BY ROBOTS.

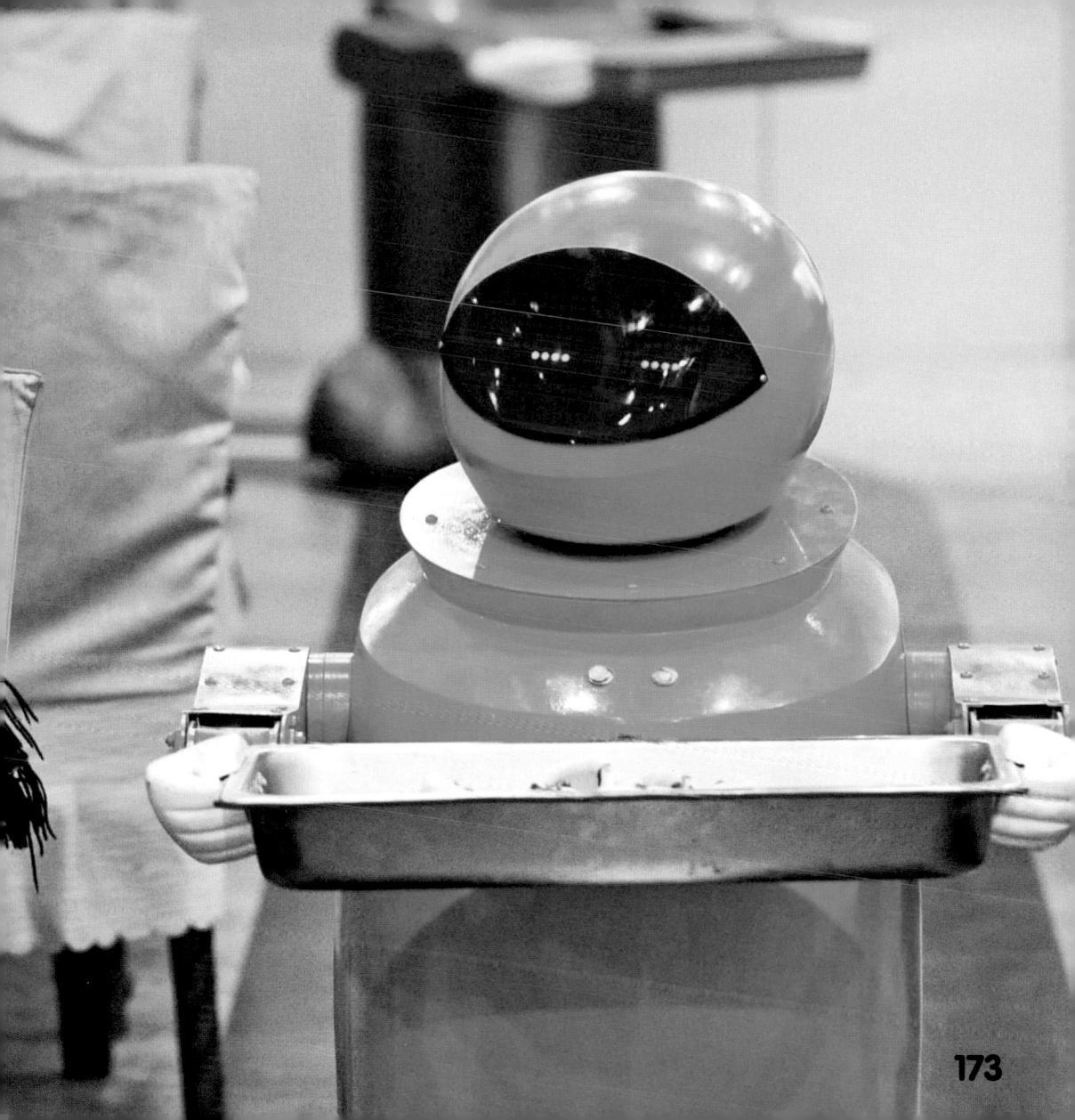

RADISHES ARE A COMMON BREAKFAST FOOD IN JAPAN.

CHOPSTICKS WERE INVENTED

MORE THAN 4,000 YEARS AGO.

PEOPLE USED TO BELIEVE EATING
PUMPKIN COULD REMOVE FRECKLES.

ONE OUT OF FIVE AMERICANS HAS EATEN AN ENTIRE PIE BY THEMSELVES.

THE WORLD'S LARGEST GINGERBREAD VILLAGE REQUIRED **2,240 POUNDS** (1,016 kg) OF ICING, **400 POUNDS** (181 kg) OF CANDY, AND **500 POUNDS** (227 kg) OF DOUGH.

AT ONE LONDON
CAFE,
FOOD AND DRINKS
ARE FREE,
BUT YOU
ARE CHARGED
5 CENTS
FOR EVERY
MINUTE YOU SIT.

YOU TYPICALLY
AROUND
250 TIMES
DURING A
MEAL.

SOME RASPBERRIES ARE PURPLE!

YOU CAN'T MAKE FRENCH FRIES IN SPACE.

ALMOST HALF OF A MOVIE THEATER'S PROFITS ARE MADE FROM SELLING SNACKS.

MILLIONS OF YEARS AGO, GIANT GROUND SLOTHS ATE AVOCADOS.

Jackfruit—the largest fruit to grow on a tree—can weigh more than four watermelons.

COMPETITORS
AT THE WORLD
PEA SHOOTING
CHAMPIONSHIPS
IN ENGLAND BLAST PEAS
THROUGH BLOWPIPES
AT TARGETS.

One ice-cream truck in New York City offers a "Godzilla" cone—vanilla ice cream covered in crushed spicy wasabi peas.

SOME BANANAS HAVE

RED SKINS

PINK FLESH—

YET TASTE THE SAME AS THE YELLOW KIND.

73% of home cooks admit to licking the spoon.

BRITISH ROYALS ONCE SERVED SWAN AT SPECIAL BANQUETS.

A restaurant in Budapest, Hungary, offers nearly 2,000 items on its menu.

A company in England will print your photos on marshmallows.

You can order
a "milkshake burger"
—a cheeseburger topped
with deep-fried ice cream—
in Florida, U.S.A.

Macaroni and Cheese,
Asparagus,
and Cotton Candy
are not only foods;
they're also crayon colors.

Some ancient Greeks and Romans believed that smelling basil would cause scorpions to grow in their brains.

Ancient Egyptians ate ham and eggs for breakfast more than 3,000 years ago.

A can of jellied cranberry sauce contains about 200 cranberries.

The Japanese tradition of **eating pufferfish**—one of the world's most poisonous fish—**kills five people** every year.

DON'T EVEN THINK ABOUT IT!

EARLY MOVIE THEATERS BANNED POPCORN BECAUSE IT WAS TOO MESSY.

U.S. PRESIDENT
THOMAS JEFFERSON SERVED
MACARONI AND CHEESE
AT A STATE DINNER.

DURING WORLD WAR II, KIDS WERE OFFERED

CARROTS-ON-A-STICK

INSTEAD OF ICE CREAM.

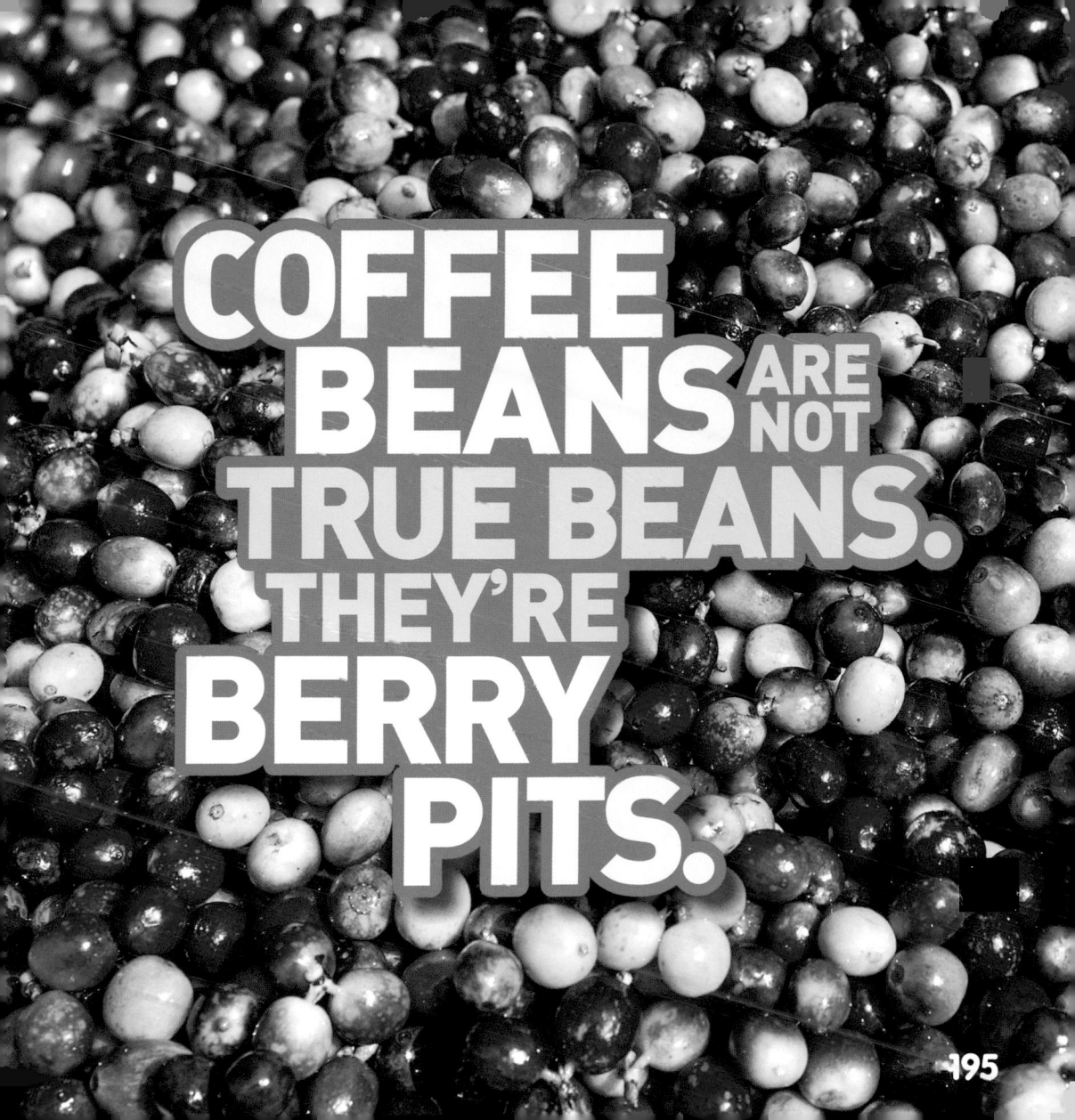
COFFEE
BEANS ARE NOT
TRUE BEANS.
THEY'RE
BERRY
PITS.

IN OHIO, U.S.A., THERE ARE

109 SIX-FOOT-TALL

(1.8 m)

CONCRETE EARS OF CORN
STANDING IN ROWS IN A FORMER CORNFIELD.

THAT'S WEIRD!
The world's heaviest watermelon weighed as much as 10 koalas!

A GERMAN DESIGN COMPANY **MADE A COOKBOOK** ENTIRELY OUT OF **FRESH PASTA,** SO YOU CAN **READ IT, COOK IT, AND *EAT IT*.**

FACTFINDER

Illustrations are indicated by **boldface.**

A

Airplane travel 120, **120**
Aldrin, Buzz 37
Alektorophobia 81
Anchovies 27
Apple cider 97
Apple pie 16, **16–17**
Apples 97, 158, **158**
Apricots 19, **19**
Arcimboldo, Giuseppe 164
Arizona, U.S.A. 38, 138
Armstrong, Neil 37
Art 156, **156,** 160, 164, **164**
Asparagus 163, **163,** 188
Astronauts *see* Space travel
Australia 18, **18,** 86
Avocados **136,** 136–137, 181

B

Babies, dressed like burritos 6, **6**
Bacon 103, **103,** 168, **168**
Baconnaise 139
Bacteria 100, 104
Bagels 25, **25,** 39
Balsamic vinegar 122
Bananas **136–137**
    banana-flavored confetti 59
    color 184, **184–185**
    genetics 137
    "mock bananas" 43
    nutrition 136–137
    peels 2, **2**
    stickers 136
Barbecuing, as protest 93, **93**
Barbie Cafe, Taipei, Taiwan 66, **66**
Barnesville, Minnesota, U.S.A. 51, **51**
Basil 189, **189**
Baskin-Robbins 115, **115**
Beans 8, 33, **33,** 61
Ben and Jerry's 25
Berrien Springs, Michigan, U.S.A. 79
Bicycles 122, **122**
Black pepper 49
Black pudding 24, **24**
Bolt, Usain 33
Borscht 43
Bowls, edible 159, **159**
Brazil 93, **93**
Bread 80, 92, **92,** 110, 170, **170**
Breakfast 54, **54,** 103, 174
    see also Cereal
Brussels kale 154–155, **155**
Brussels sprouts **154,** 154–155
Bubble gum 56, **56**
Budapest, Hungary 186
Burger King 60
Burps, world's loudest 147
Burritos, babies dressed as 6, **6**
Butter 31, 57, **57,** 103

C

Cabbages, world's largest 26, **26**
Cakes 16, **16–17,** 67, **67,** 144, **144**
California, U.S.A. 120, 122, **122,** 152
Calories 120, 138, 141
Cambodia 115, **115**
Campfires 52, **52–53**
Canada 63, **63,** 138, **138**
Candles 165, **165**
Candy
    bacteria in 104
    candy canes 90, **90**
    chocolate 111, **111, 118,** 119, 132
    Dum Dum lollipops 129
    gummy candy 72, **72,** 132
    jelly beans 152, **152**
    Snickers bars 132
    Sweethearts 78, **78**
Caramel 85
Cardboard 44, **44**
Carolina Reaper chili 45, **45**
Carrots
    as decoration 104, **104**
    as ice cream replacement 194
    nutrition 74, **74**
    world's longest 147, **147**
Cashew nuts 42
Casu marzu (cheese) 50
Caterpillars 84, **84**
Cats 149, **149**
Cavity prevention 104, 135, **135**
Celery 27, **27,** 62, **62**
Cereal
    1970s 75, **75**
    amount consumed 153
    Cheerios 102, **102**
    Froot Loops **88–89,** 89
    Lucky Charms 116, **116**
    Rice Krispies 18, **18,** 175
Chandeliers 72, **72,** 123, **123**
Cheerios 102, **102**
Cheese
    blue cheese 100
    brine to thaw roads 140, **140**
    buried with the dead 147, **147**
    as cavity fighter 135, **135**
    craved by Americans 9, **9**
    fear of 115
    as presidential gift 61, **61**
    in "walking taco" 135, **135**
Cheetos 105, **105**
Chef's hats 50, **50**
Chelsea soccer club 62, **62**
Cherimoya 56, **56**

Cherpumple 16, **16–17**
Cherries 85
Cherry blossoms 127, 168
Cherry pie 16, **16–17**
Chicago White Sox 135
Chicken
    chicken nuggets 90
    in cibero 30
    in corsages 13, **13**
    eggs 98, **98**
    fear of 81
    in gooducken 103
    mushrooms tasting like **82–83,** 83
    in Tudor Christmas Pie 114
Chili 135, **135**
Chili peppers 45, **45,** 57, 132
China
    ancient China 147
    chilies to cure headaches 57
    chopsticks 54
    cloud ears (mushrooms) 128
    noodles 73, **73**
    restaurants 172, **172–173**
Chiquita bananas 136
Chocolate 111, **111, 118,** 119, 132
Chocolate-covered bacon 168, **168**
Chopsticks 54, 159, **159,** 174–175, **174–175**
Christmas foods 54, 87, **87,** 114
Chyme 25
Cibero 30
Clam strips 61
Cloud ears (mushrooms) 128
Coca-Cola 126
Cockscombs 30
Coconut crabs **4–5,** 5
Coconut shells 123, **123**
Coconut water 138
Coconuts 5, **5,** 105
Coffee **130–131**
    beans 195, **195**
    coffee shops 130, 131
    freeze-dried 25
    Starbucks 130–131
    as valuable commodity 36, **36**
Colds, fought by garlic 8, **8**
Colonial era 165
Color
    bananas 184, **184–185**
    bread twist tie 92, **92**
    crayon colors 188, **188**
    effect on senses 81, **81**
    fading prevention 49
    Froot Loops **88–89,** 89
    gummy candy 132
    hunger and 151, **151**
    orange 80
    sweet potatoes 166, **166–167**
Columbus, Christopher 168
Cookbooks 135, 199, **199**
Cookies 27, **27,** 63, **63,** 126, 162
Corn dogs 138
Corn statues 196–197, **196–197**
Corsages, fried chicken in 13, **13**
Cotton candy 108, 188
Cows 39, 117
Crab legs 61
Cranberries 8, **8,** 57, **57**
Cranberry sauce 189, **189**
Cravings 9, **9**
Crayon colors 188, **188**
Crisphead 36, **36**
Crogels 39, **39**
Croissants 39
Crum, George 162
Cupcakes 30, **30**
Cupuaçu (fruit) 43, **43**

D

Davey Jones Locker Challenge 61
Dehydrated potatoes 104
Diamonds 144, **144**
Digestion 25, 96, **96**
Dill-pickle-flavored candy canes 90, **90**
Dillsburg, Pennsylvania, U.S.A. 58
Dippin' Dots ice cream 97
Dishes 91, **91,** 99, **99,** 159, **159**
Disney theme parks 127, **127,** 158, **158**
Dogs 148, **148**
Donuts 68, **68,** 138, **138,** 194, **194**
Drinking water 142, **142–143**
Dubble Bubble gum 109
Duck, in gooducken 103
Duffins 68, **68**
Dulse (seaweed) 63, **63**
Dum Dum lollipops 129

E

Earlton, New York, U.S.A. 152
Easter candy 146, **146,** 152, **152**
Edible tattoos 42, **42**
Eel-flavored soda 180, **180**
Eggs
    as breakfast food 189
    chef's hat and 50, **50**
    hard-boiling 98, **98**
    in pound cake 31
    in shampoo 183, **183**
Egypt, ancient 90, 165, 189
Embalming 90
Engastration 63
England 104, **104,** 182, 186

F
Fast-food meals 21, **21,** 60, **60,** 127, 141
Ferrets 38, **38**
Fiddlehead ferns 114, **114**
Finland 63, **63**
Fish 36, **36,** 61, 105, 138
Fleer Company 109
Floor, food dropped on 133
Florida, U.S.A. 187, **187**
Flour, in pound cake 31
Food neophobia 120
Forks 62, **62,** 117
Freakies (cereal) 75
Freckles 176
Freeze-dried foods 25
French fries 48, **48,** 157, 181
Fried chicken 13, **13,** 87, **87**
Fritos, in "walking taco" 135, **135**
Froot Loops **88–89,** 89
Fruit, edible tattoos on 42, **42**
Fruit Smack 50

G
Garlic 8, **8**
Gas, passing 105, **105**
Geese 103, 114
Germany 59, 199, **199**
Gingerbread cookies 63, **63**
Gingerbread houses 112, **112–113,** 160, 178, **178–179**
Girl Scout cookies 162
Glücksbringer 59, **59**
"Godzilla" ice-cream cone 183, **183**
Gold 30, **30,** 152
Gooducken 103
Goose 103, 114
Grapes 9, **9,** 58, **58**
Greece, ancient 153, 189, **189**
Greenland 54
Grilled cheese sandwiches 194, **194**
Gum 80, 109
Gummy candy 72, **72,** 132

H
Haggis-hurling competition 74
Ham, as breakfast food 189
Ham-salad sandwiches 37
Hamburgers
  candles smelling like 165, **165**
  invention of 135
  from lab-grown meat 108
  milkshake burgers 187, **187**
  "Ninja Burger" 60, **60**
  shot to tables 162
Hawaii, U.S.A. 105, **105**
Headaches, cures for 57
Hershey's Kisses 111, **111**
Hiccups, cures for 153
Hot dogs 48, **48,** 120
Human body
  ancient beliefs 189, **189**
  bad breath 45, **45**
  blood plasma substitute 138
  body temperature 6
  cavity prevention 104, 135, **135**
  digestion 25, 96, **96**
  hair removal 85
  headache cure 57
  memory improvement 42, **42**
  small intestine 96, **96**
  stomach ailment cure 80, **80**
  stomach capacity 31
  sweat and urine 142, **142–143**
  sweaty feet 100, **100–101**
  taste buds 34–35, **34–35**
Hunger, color and 151, **151**

I
Ice cream
  carrots as replacement for 194
  churning 122, **122**
  Dippin' Dots 97
  flavors 115, **115,** 138, 168
  glowing 103
  "Godzilla" cone 183, **183**
  plant-based 33, **33**
  raising body temperature 6
Iceberg lettuce 36, **36**
Instant Ramen Museum, Osaka, Japan 145
Israel 129, 156, **156**
Italy 50, 110

J
Jackfruit 181
Jackson, Andrew 39
James and the Giant Peach (Dahl) 121
Japan
  edible dishes 159, **159**
  food flavors 105, **105,** 168, 180, **180**
  Instant Ramen Museum 145
  pufferfish 190, **191**
  radishes as breakfast food 174
  restaurants 60, 87, **87,** 124, **124–125,** 127
  watermelon cooler 55, **55**
Jeans, scratch-and-sniff 69, **69**
Jefferson, Thomas 61, 193
Jell-O 27, **27**
Jelly beans 152, **152**
Jellyfish 103
Jewelry, from potatoes 104

K

Kaboom (cereal) 75
Kale 154–155, **154–155**
Kentucky Fried Chicken (KFC) 13, **13,** 87, **87**
Ketchup
  as ice cream flavor 115, **115**
  "no ketchup" rule 135
  squirting speed 33
  for stomach ailments 80, **80**
  tomatoes in **22–23,** 23
KFC (Kentucky Fried Chicken) 13, **13,** 87, **87**
Kidney beans 33, **33**
Kiribati (island) 105
Kiwis 129, **129**
Knives 117
Knorks 117
Kool-Aid 50
Kumquats 7, **7**

L

Laetiporus mushrooms **82–83,** 83
Langue de chat 27, **27**
Laser-guided pizza cutter 162
Laundry 49, **49**
Lemons 106, **106–107,** 129
Lettuce 36, **36**
Lickable wallpaper 126
Limequats 7, **7**
Limes 7, **7**
London, England 59, 126, 180
Los Angeles, California, U.S.A. 79
Louvre, Paris, France 160, **160–161**
Lucky Charms 116, **116**

M

Macaroni and cheese 188, 193
Maggots, in cheese 50
Maldive Islands 94, **94–95**
Mangoes 157
Marathons 141
"Marbits" 116, **116**
Marshmallows 116, **116,** 146, **146,** 186
Marzipan 59, **59**
Mashed potatoes 51, **51,** 145
Mayonnaise 15, **15,** 139
McDonald's 21, **21,** 127
Meat 76, **76–77,** 129
Meatless Mondays 79
"Melon skiers" 86
Microwaves 9, **9**
Middle Ages 15, **15**
Milk 117
Milkshake burgers 187, **187**
Mint 69, **69,** 153
"Miracle berry" 104
Mobile, Alabama, U.S.A. 58
Moby-Dick (Melville) 130–131
Mock food 43
Modernist Cuisine (cookbook) 135
Moon, sandwiches eaten on 37
Moon Pies 58
Mopane worms 84, **84**
Mountain Dew, as flavor 105, **105**
Movie theaters 181, 192
Muffins 68, **68**
Muktuk 54
Mushrooms 20, **20, 82–83,** 83, 128
Music 12, 14, **14**
Mussels 61
Mycophobia 20, **20**

N

Neanderthals 134, **134**
New England, U.S.A. 114, **114**
New Jersey, U.S.A. 150, **150**
New Year celebrations 58–59, **58–59**
New York, New York, U.S.A. 61, 171, 183, **183**
New Zealand 162
Night of the Radishes 28, **28–29**
Nightmares 15, **15**
Nike running shoes 54
"Ninja Burger" 60, **60**
Noodles 73, **73,** 145
Norway 57, **57**
Nutella 6

O

Oatmeal 24
Oaxaca, Mexico 28, **28–29**
Octopus 10, **10–11**
Ohio, U.S.A. 194, 196–197, **196–197**
Oil 36
Olives 40, **40–41**
Olympic Games 43
Onions 149, **149,** 165
Orange (color) 80
Oranges (fruit) 52, **52–53,** 80
Orchids, deep-fried 174, **174**
Oreo vending machine 153, **153**
Osaka, Japan 145
Ostrich eggs 98, **98**
Oxfordshire, England 80
Oysters 153

P

Partridges 114
Pasta 199, **199**
Pea shooting 182
Peaches 121, **121**
Peanut butter and jelly sandwiches 114, **114**
Peanuts 115

Peeps (candy) 146, **146**
Peppers 45, **45,** 49, 57
Pets Deli, Berlin, Germany 97
Philadelphia, Pennsylvania, U.S.A. 76, **76–77,** 103, **103**
Philippines 123, **123**
Phobias 20, **20,** 81, 115, 120
Photography, of meat 76, **76–77**
Pickles 58, 79, **79,** 168, **168**
Pies
  cherpumple 16, **16–17**
  eaten by one person 177, **177**
  largest pumpkin pie 70, **70–71**
  in Tudor Christmas Pie 114
Pigeons 114
Pigs 24, 59, **59,** 64, **64–65**
Pillsbury Doughboy 129
Pineapples 165
Pistachios 157
Pizza
  calories in 120
  laser-guided cutter 162
  in space 14, **14**
  storage temperature 157
  toppings 81, **81**
  world records 145, **145**
Plates 91, **91,** 159, **159**
Poison ivy 157
Poisonous foods 148, **148,** 149, **149,** 190, **191**
Pop (soda) 110, **110,** 126, 180, **180**
Popcorn 192, **192**
Poppin' Fresh, and family 129
Popsicles 105, **105**
Potato chips 162, **162**
Potatoes 51, **51,** 104, 145, 152
Pound cakes 31
Price, Vincent 32, **32**
Prom season 13, **13**
Pudding 24, **24,** 74
Pufferfish 190, **191**
Pumpkin donuts 171
Pumpkin pie 16, **16–17,** 70, **70–71**
Pumpkins 176, **176**

Q
Quisp (cereal) 75

R
Radishes 28, **28–29,** 90, 174
Rambutan (fruit) 139, **139**
Ramen noodles 145
Rashes 42
Raspberries 181
Red (color) 132, **132,** 151, **151**
Refried beans 8
Restaurants
  Barbie Cafe 66, **66**
  Burger King 60
  cardboard furniture 44, **44**
  coffee shops 130–131
  Davey Jones Locker Challenge 61
  ferret prohibition 38, **38**
  free food and drink 180
  giant stuffed animals 124, **124–125**
  large menu 186
  McDonald's 21, **21,** 127
  "no ketchup" rule 135
  Pets Deli 97
  Robot Restaurant 172, **172–173**
  shooting burgers to tables 162
  underwater 94, **94–95**
  wait list 152
Rhubarb 148, **148**
Rice Bubbles 18, **18**
Rice Krispies 18, **18,** 175
Richterswil, Switzerland **46–47,** 47
Robot Restaurant, China 172, **172–173**
Rome, ancient 36, 45, **45,** 189, **189**
Rome, Italy 138
Rosemary 42, **42**
Running 141
Russia 43

S
Saffron 171, **171**
Salmon 138
Salty flavors 120, **120,** 157
Sandwiches 37, 114, **114,** 194, **194**
Sannakji 10, **10–11**
Sausage 24
Scents
  from bacteria 100, **100–101**
  coffee shops 131
  hamburger candles 165, **165**
  from smartphone 93, **93**
Scotland 74
Scratch-and-sniff jeans 69, **69**
Seattle, Washington, U.S.A. 130
Seaweed 63, **63**
Shampoo 183, **183**
Shoe treads 54, **54**
Shrimp 61
Silverware 117
Singapore 80, 145
Small intestine 96, **96**
Smartphones 93, **93**
Smoked-salmon gelato 138
Snickers bars 132
Soccer 62, **62**
Soda 110, **110,** 126, 180, **180**
Sole (fish) 36, **36**
Sour food 104

South Korea 48, **48**
Space travel
3-D printing of meals 12
french fries 181
pizza 14, **14**
recycled sweat and urine 142, **142–143**
sandwiches eaten on moon 37
velcro dishes 99, **99**
Spain 58, **58**
Spam, as flavor 105, **105**
Spices 171, **171**
Spicy foods 139
Spifes 117
Spoons 117, 150, **150**, 186, **186**
Sporks 117
Starbucks Coffee 130–131
Stomach ailments 80, **80**
Stomach capacity 31
Strawberries 45, **45**, 174, **174**
Street food 48, **48**
Sugar 31, 43
Swallowing 180
Swans 186
Sweat 100, **100–101**, 142, **142–143**
Sweet flavors 12, 104, 120, **120**, 157
Sweet potatoes 104, 166, **166–167**, 168
Sweethearts (candy) 78, **78**

T

Tacos 103, **103**, 135, **135**
Taipei, Taiwan 66, **66**
Taiwan 44, **44**, 66, **66**
Tarantulas, deep-fried 115, **115**
Taste buds 34–35, **34–35**, 104
Tattoos, edible 42, **42**
Thailand 174, **174**
Thanksgiving foods 120, 171
Thin Mints 162
3-D printing 12, 153, **153**
Thyme 15, **15**
Tomatoes
in ketchup **22–23**, 23
in nightshade family 12, **12**
origin 132
world's heaviest 169, **169**
Toothpacks 168
"Tortilla Baby" 6, **6**
Truffles 64, **64–65**
Tudor Christmas Pie 114
Turkey 114, 127, **127**, 171
Turnips 30, **30**, 43, 46, **46–47**
Turophobia 115

U

Underwater restaurant 94, **94–95**
United Kingdom 24, **24**, 103, 144, **144**, 157
United States
ban on sliced bread 170, **170**
colonial era 165
Disney theme parks 127, **127**
food cravings 9, **9**
food varieties 165
peanut butter and jelly sandwiches 114, **114**
pepperoni pizzas 81, **81**
pie consumption 177, **177**
Thanksgiving 120
time spent eating and drinking 126
Urine, recycling 142, **142–143**
U.S. Army 157

V

Velcro dishes 99, **99**
Vending machines 145, 153, **153**
Vinegar 27, 122

W

Waffles 54, **54**
Wallpaper, lickable 126
Walt Disney World, Orlando, Florida, U.S.A. 158, **158**
Wasabi 90, **90**, 183, **183**
Water 142, **142–143**
Watermelons 55, **55**, 86, 198, **198**
Wedding cakes 67, **67**, 144, **144**
Whales, as food 54
White House, Washington, D.C., U.S.A. 39, 112, **112–113**, 193
William, Prince 67
Wisconsin, U.S.A. 140, **140**, 168, **168**
Worcestershire sauce 27
World War II 43, 194

Y

Yams 104
Yardlong (bean) 61

Z

Zucchinis 20, **20**

Published by National Geographic Partners, LLC.

Copyright © 2015 National Geographic Society. All rights reserved. Reproduction of the whole or any part of the contents without written permission from the publisher is prohibited.

NATIONAL GEOGRAPHIC and Yellow Border Design are trademarks of the National Geographic Society, used under license.

Since 1888, the National Geographic Society has funded more than 14,000 research, conservation, education, and storytelling projects around the world. National Geographic Partners distributes a portion of the funds it receives from your purchase to National Geographic Society to support programs including the conservation of animals and their habitats. To learn more, visit natgeo.com/info.

For more information, visit nationalgeographic.com, call 1-877-873-6846, or write to the following address:

National Geographic Partners, LLC
1145 17th Street NW
Washington, DC 20036-4688 U.S.A.

For librarians and teachers: nationalgeographic.com/books/librarians-and-educators

More for kids from National Geographic: natgeokids.com

For rights or permissions inquiries, please contact National Geographic Books Subsidiary Rights: bookrights@natgeo.com

Paperback ISBN: 978-1-4263-1871-9
Reinforced Library Binding ISBN: 978-1-4263-1872-6

Printed in Hong Kong
23/PPHK/6 (PB)
23/PPHK/4 (RLB)

Staff for This Book
Amy Briggs, *Project Manager*
Rebecca Baines, *Project Editor*
Julide Obuz Dengel, *Art Director*
Hillary Leo, *Photo Editor*
Rachael Hamm Plett, Moduza Design, *Designer*
Paige Towler, *Editorial Assistant*
Julie Beer and Sarah Wassner, *Researchers*
Allie Allen and Sanjida Rashid, *Design Production Assistants*
Michael Cassady, *Photo Assistant*
Michael Libonati, *Special Projects Assistant*
Grace Hill, *Associate Managing Editor*
Mike O'Connor, *Production Editor*
Lewis R. Bassford, *Production Manager*
Nicole Elliott, *Director of Production*
Susan Borke, *Legal and Business Affairs*

Senior Management Team, Kids Publishing and Media
Nancy Laties Feresten, *Senior Vice President;* Jennifer Emmett, *Vice President, Editorial Director, Kids Books;* Julie Vosburgh Agnone, *Vice President, Editorial Operations;* Rachel Buchholz, *Editor and Vice President,* NG Kids *magazine;* Michelle Sullivan, *Vice President, Kids Digital;* Eva Absher-Schantz, *Design Director;* Jay Sumner, *Photo Director;* Hannah August, *Marketing Director;* R. Gary Colbert, *Production Director*

Digital Anne McCormack, *Director;* Laura Goertzel, Sara Zeglin, *Producers;* Jed Winer, *Special Projects Assistant;* Emma Rigney, *Creative Producer;* Brian Ford, *Video Producer;* Bianca Bowman, *Assistant Producer;* Natalie Jones, *Senior Product Manager*

Based on the "Weird But True" department in *National Geographic Kids* magazine

ALL ARTWORK BY MODUZA DESIGN UNLESS OTHERWISE NOTED BELOW:

COVER AND SPINE, FLICKR RM/GETTY IMAGES; 2, FLICKR RM/GETTY IMAGES; 4-5, STEPHEN BELCHER/MINDEN PICTURES; 5, EVGENY KARANDAEV/SHUTTERSTOCK; 6, COURTESY OF BON VIVANT BABY, LLC; 8(UP), CISCA CASTELLINS/NIS/MINDEN PICTURES; 8(LO), ALESSANDRO GUERRIERO/SHUTTERSTOCK; 9(LE), TETRA IMAGES/ALAMY; 9(RT), MAU HORNG/SHUTTERSTOCK; 10-11, TRAVEL IMAGES/ALAMY; 13, POLARIS/NEWSCOM; 14, COURTESY OF ANAMANAGUCHI; 15(LE), ISTOCKPHOTO; 15(RT), FENG YU/SHUTTERSTOCK; 16-17, CHARLES PHOENIX; 18, JOSEPH GARERI/GETTY IMAGES; 19, ISTOCKPHOTO; 22-23, TIGERGALLERY/SHUTTERSTOCK; 25, MADLEN/SHUTTERSTOCK; 26, VLADIMIR ILIEVSKI/SHUTTERSTOCK; 28-29, ROBERT FRERCK/GETTY IMAGES; 30(LE), SPLASH NEWS/NEWSCOM; 30(RT), AFRICA STUDIO/SHUTTERSTOCK; 32, AF ARCHIVE/ALAMY; 33, KIM NGUYEN/SHUTTERSTOCK; 34-35, PRINCESSDLAF/ISTOCKPHOTO; 36, KIM NGUYEN/SHUTTERSTOCK; 38, JAGODKA/SHUTTERSTOCK; 39, COURTESY STEW LEONARD'S; 40-41, AE PICTURES INC./GETTY IMAGES; 43, AGE FOTOSTOCK SPAIN, S.L./ALAMY; 44, STILLFX/SHUTTERSTOCK; 45, COURTESY PUCKER BUTT PEPPER COMPANY; 46, EPA/NEWSCOM; 47, EPA/NEWSCOM; 48, ERIC J. OLSEN; 50(BACK), YANG NA/SHUTTERSTOCK; 50,(FRONT) APPLY PICTURES/ALAMY; 51, COURTESY OF BARNESVILLE RECORD REVIEW; 52, TIM UR/SHUTTERSTOCK; 52-53, TERO HAKALA/SHUTTERSTOCK; 54, UMLAUT1968/SHUTTERSTOCK; 56, TIMABBOTT/ISTOCKPHOTO; 57, SOMMAI/SHUTTERSTOCK; 58-59, ENCIKAN/SHUTTERSTOCK; 58, ALEXANDER DASHEWSKY/SHUTTERSTOCK; 59, PICTURE-ALLIANCE/NEWSCOM; 62, PHOTODISC; 63(LE), MADLEN/SHUTTERSTOCK; 63(RT), CHUCK PLACE/ALAMY; 64-65, BLOOMBERG NEWS/GETTY IMAGES; 67, AFP/GETTY IMAGES; 69, WENN.COM/NEWSCOM; 70-71, WENN.COM/NEWSCOM, 72, KEVIN CHAMPENY; 76-77, DOMINIC EPISCOPO; 81, IRES003/SHUTTERSTOCK; 82-83, KURKUL/ISTOCKPHOTO; 84, KIM TAYLOR/MINDEN PICTURES; 88-89, GUZEL STUDIO/SHUTTERSTOCK; 94-95, CONRAD MALDIVES RANGALI ISLAND; 96, RAYCAT/ISTOCKPHOTO; 98, JIRI HERA/SHUTTERSTOCK; 100-101, PESKYMONKEY/ISTOCKPHOTO; 103 COURTESY PYT BURGER & BAR; 104, NATTIKA/SHUTTERSTOCK; 106-107, VICTORIA ROMANCHENKO/SHUTTERSTOCK; 111, WIREIMAGE/GETTY IMAGES; 112-113, AFP/GETTY IMAGES; 118, DREAMSTIME; 123, JAMES HOAGLAND; 124-125, XPERIANE/FLICKR; 129, GOODSHOOT; 130-131, LOSKUTNIKOV/SHUTTERSTOCK; 130, 3PLUSX/SHUTTERSTOCK; 131, MAGICOVEN/SHUTTERSTOCK; 136-137, MAZZZUR/SHUTTERSTOCK; 136, SAI0112/SHUTTERSTOCK; 139, TAWEESAK THIPROD/SHUTTERSTOCK; 142-143, NASA; 145, D. HURST/ALAMY; 148, ONEINCHPUNCH/SHUTTERSTOCK; 149, THEPROPSHOPPE/ISTOCKPHOTO; 152, DANIEL WIEDEMANN/SHUTTERSTOCK; 153, OLGA POPOVA/SHUTTERSTOCK; 154(LE), PETER ZIJLSTRA/SHUTTERSTOCK; 154(RT), KIM NGUYEN/SHUTTERSTOCK; 155, KALETTES/SCOTT KNUTSON; 156, SHAY AARON; 159, COURTESY RICE-DESIGN, NOBUHIKO ARIKAWA; 160-161, PATRICK WANG/SHUTTERSTOCK; 160 (LICORICE), LISINSKI/ISTOCKPHOTO; 160(CANDIES), THECRIMSONMONKEY/ISTOCKPHOTO; 164, IMAGNO/AUSTRIAN ARCHIVES/HULTON FINE ART COLLECTION/GETTY IMAGES; 166-167, PHLOEN/ALAMY; 171, MARCO SPERANZA/SHUTTERSTOCK; 172-173, WANG JIANWEI/XINHUA/SIPA USA/NEWSCOM; 176, SEB29/ISTOCKPHOTO; 177, STUDIOSOURCE/ALAMY; 178-179, EPA/NEWSCOM; 181, HXDBZXY/SHUTTERSTOCK; 183, FELICIA CHEN; 184-185, DBIMAGES/ALAMY; 190-191, DAVID FLEETHAM/ALAMY; 195, PUMPUJA/ISTOCKPHOTO; 196-197, TIM PORDIE; 198(UP), ERIC ISSELEE/SHUTTERSTOCK; 198(LO), LEONID KARCHEVSKY/ISTOCKPHOTO; 198-199, JIRI HERA/SHUTTERSTOCK; 199, PHOTOGRAPHER, JAN BURWICK/STYLIST, CHRISTOPH HIMMEL

If you LiKED this book, you'll also love the National Geographic KIDS ALMANAC.

Available wherever books are sold.

PLAY with your FOOD!

See what WEIRD, FUN, and YUMMY treats you can create with this awesome cookbook, especially for YOU!

Play With Your Food!

Snow day snacks are the perfect way to crack up while you fuel up! Now that you know how to make some of my favorite snow day snacks—like Dinosaur Kale Chips and Ants on a Log—your challenge is to come up with your own creative concoction. See if you can make edible caterpillars (hint: start with a banana), cauliflower sheep, or marshmallow snowmen. Even better, grab a friend or family member, and create his or her likeness out of fruit and veggies!

Marshmallow Snowmen

When it's too cold to make real snowmen outside, try making some edible versions in front of a toasty fire. These guys are the ultimate way to have fun with your food—and they're easy to make! Marshmallows will harden when left out, so they make cute wintery decorations ... or you can just eat them right away, of course.

Prep: about 5 minutes, or as long as you want

Marshmallows (try using different sizes, like jumbo, regular, and mini)

Toothpicks

Frosting

Candy for decorating—I use M&Ms and Red Hots, but your imagination is the limit!

1. Assemble your snowman, using the marshmallows and toothpicks. You can use different sizes for the body, head, and arms, or do whatever you like!
2. Now decorate your snowman! You can use pretzels for arms, licorice for candy scarves, candy for hats, or whatever else you can dream up. Frosting helps secure the candy to the marshmallows.
3. You're finished! You can display your snowman as awesome snowy decorations, play with them, or eat them. If you decide to unlock on your creations, just make sure to remove the toothpicks first.

KITCHEN SKILL

How to Use a Knife Knife skills are absolutely essential for any cook. The first skill to learn when using a knife is how to not cut yourself! Always be conscious of the knife and how you hold it. Never point with a knife, and when walking with a knife, make sure that the tip is always pointing down. A sharp knife is absolutely essential. Here's why: A knife is a tool meant to do the work for you. A sharp knife slides right through food, making a clean and easy cut. Dull knives won't cut so easily and therefore require the chef to use pressure to attempt to force the knife through the ingredient. When you exert pressure, you can lose control, and the knife can slip and cut you. Get a sharp knife and let the knife do the work for you!

Another important thing to remember is that you are trying to cut the food—not yourself—so keep your fingers protected. The best way to do this is to grip the item to be cut with your fingers curled inward so that the knife can lean against your knuckle. This not only helps guide the knife to cut where you want it to, but it also keeps your fingertips safely away from the blade.

20 JANUARY

JANUARY 21

© 2015 National Geographic Society

AVAILABLE WHEREVER BOOKS ARE SOLD
Discover more at kids.nationalgeographic.com

NATIONAL GEOGRAPHIC KIDS